the simplicity of HEARING God
21 ways God speaks to us

Capazin Thornton

The Simplicity of Hearing God
21 Ways God Speaks to Us

Copyright © 2020 Capazin Thornton

ALL RIGHTS RESERVED. No portion of this book may be reproduced, stored in a retrieval system, or transmitted in any form or by any means—electronic, mechanical, photocopy, recording, scanning, or other—except for brief quotations in critical reviews or articles, without the prior written permission of the author/publisher.

All Scripture quotations, unless otherwise indicated, are taken from the New King James Version®. Copyright © 1982 by Thomas Nelson. Used by permission. All rights reserved.

Scripture quotations marked TPT are from The Passion Translation®. Copyright © 2017, 2018 by Passion & Fire Ministries, Inc. Used by permission. All rights reserved. ThePassionTranslation.com.

Scripture quotations marked ICB are from the International Children's Bible® (ICB) Copyright© 1986, 1988, 1999, 2015 by Tommy Nelson™, a division of Thomas Nelson. Used by permission.

Scripture quotations marked NLT are from the New Living Translation (NLT), copyright © 1996, 2004, 2015 by Tyndale House Foundation. Used by permission of Tyndale House Publishers, Inc., Carol Stream, Illinois 60188.

Scripture quotations marked ISV are from the International Standard Version (ISV) Copyright © 1995-2014 by ISV Foundation. ALL RIGHTS RESERVED INTERNATIONALLY.

The Simplicity of Hearing God
21 Ways God Speaks to Us
by Capazin Thornton
Copyright © 2020
ISBN: 978-0-9755473-5-9

Printed in the United States of America

To learn more about and/or request other publications by Capazin Thornton, please visit the website: https://capazin.com

Dedicated to all who want to discover more
about the many ways God speaks to us

CONTENTS

	Introduction	1
Chapter 1	Holy Scriptures	3
Chapter 2	Jesus Christ	13
Chapter 3	Conscience	19
Chapter 4	Intuition	23
Chapter 5	Communion	27
Chapter 6	Still Small Voice	31
Chapter 7	Holy Spirit, the Anointing	35
Chapter 8	Audible Voice of the Lord	41
Chapter 9	Fruit of the Spirit	45
Chapter 10	Word of Wisdom	49
Chapter 11	Word of Knowledge	53
Chapter 12	Discerning of Spirits	59
Chapter 13	Prophecy	65
Chapter 14	Spiritual Languages	71

Chapter 15	Dreams and Visions	75
Chapter 16	Creative Ideas	81
Chapter 17	Rhema	83
Chapter 18	Songs	87
Chapter 19	Ministry Gifts	89
Chapter 20	Circumstances	95
Chapter 21	Angels	103
Chapter 22	Four Steps to Hearing God	109
Epilogue		115
Appendix		
Prerequisites to Hear God		A-1
About Bible Versions		A-5
How to Rightly Divide God's Word		A-7
Notes		
About the Author		

Acknowledgments

Kevin Burns (admin@netcitynet.com), a true *quid quo pro* friend, for video book trailer

Jorg Jorgenson (Agent 41), my web designer, tech genius, and friend, for his labors of love, and prayers

James L. Smith, Jr., my dear son, who always listens, reviews, constructively critiques, and in the end usually agrees with me

INTRODUCTION

God loves to talk. So, He has filled the whole universe with His voice.

Yet, people struggle to hear God and know His will.

When I grew up, it was common for people to say, "The Lord works in mysterious ways, His wonders to perform." While there may be some truth in that statement, I now believe such comments were an excuse to be lazy.

What do I mean? Instead of seeking to hear God for ourselves, we settled for what other people told us about God and what they thought He was saying. Unfortunately, this occurs too often today.

Friends, every person is God's unique creation. God wants each of us to know Him personally and hear His voice. No one should be able to understand what God is saying to you better than you.

So, hearing God is a big deal. But it is easier than you think.

THE SIMPLICITY OF HEARING GOD explores 21 ways God speaks to us.

You will discover:

- God put sensors in your spirit to keep you conscious of Him and sensitive to His voice.

- God speaks through the fruit of the spirit.

- He speaks through prophetic dreams and visions.

- He speaks through spiritual gifts.

- On all vital matters concerning us, God has already spoken.

- God gives creative ideas.

- God sings and rejoices.

- Four simple steps to cultivate hearing God

AND SO MUCH MORE!

With so many opportunities to become more intimately acquainted with God, dive in.

I pray that God floods your spirit with His marvelous light and truth as you discover and experience THE SIMPLICITY OF HEARING GOD: 21 Ways God Speaks to Us.

Capazin

1
HOLY SCRIPTURES

> Your word is a lamp to my feet and a light to my path. (Ps 119:105)

Did you know the main way God speaks to us is through the Holy Scriptures (the Bible)? In fact, on all vital matters, God has already spoken!

So, let's start with this key way God speaks to us.

First, know:

1. *The Scriptures are God-breathed.*

   All Scripture is given by inspiration of God, and is profitable for doctrine, for reproof, for correction, for instruction in righteousness (2 Tim 3:16)

2. *No prophecy of Scripture came by human will.*

   Above all, you must realize that no prophecy in Scripture ever came from the prophet's own understanding, or from human initiative. No, those prophets were moved by the Holy Spirit, and they spoke from God. (2 Pet 1:20-21, NLT)

The Bible is a supernatural book

Over 1500 years, across three continents, God selected and anointed 40 men to record His words. They used three main languages: Hebrew, Aramaic, and Greek.

God told Moses: "Write down these words, because I'm making a covenant with you and with Israel according to these words." And Moses wrote down all the words of the Lord. (Ex 34:27, ISV; Ex 24:4)

One time, God Himself wrote the words. "The Lord said to Moses, 'Chisel out two stone tablets like the first ones. I will write on them the same words that were on the tablets you smashed.'" (Ex 34:1, NLT)

God directed Jeremiah: "Get a scroll. Write on it all the words I have spoken to you." (Jere 36:2, ICB)

And so, all the writers penned exactly what God wanted. *Spirit-moved men produced Spirit-breathed writings*! These words from God were hand copied onto papyrus, parchment, and ultimately printed on paper. Today, the Holy Scriptures have been translated into many of the world's languages. (*See Appendix, About Bible Versions.*)

These *God-breathed* Scriptures are called:

>Word of God
>Word of Truth
>Holy Scriptures
>Word of Life
>Word of Faith
>Prophetic word made certain, and

Incorruptible seed which lives and abides forever.

(Heb 4:12; 2 Tim 2:15; Rom 1:2; 2 Pet 1:19; Phil 2:16; Rom 10:8; 1 Pet 1:23)

The Holy Scriptures are God's self-revelation

A revelation discloses things unknown. The invisible yet ever-present God speaks out from the pages of the Holy Scriptures revealing Himself, His extraordinary ways, excellent will, and tremendous works.

He reveals Himself first as Elohim ('ĕ·lō·hîm), the Creator. Elohim is a plural noun. It means *divine ones* and hints at the three-person Godhead later unveiled:

> The Spirit of Elohim was hovering or moving over the face of the waters. (Gen 1:2)
>
> Six days later, God said, "Let Us make man in Our image, according to Our likeness" (Gen 1:26).
>
> The apostle John reveals Jesus Christ as the Word, eternally with God, who Himself is God, and who made all things. (Jn 1:1-3, 14)
>
> Matthew's Gospel shows Jesus on earth, God's spirit descends on Him, and His Father speaks to Him from heaven: "When Jesus came up out of the water after being baptized, the heavens suddenly opened up, and he saw God's Spirit descending like a dove and resting on Him. And a voice came out of heaven saying, 'This is my dearly-loved Son, in whom I am well pleased.'" (Mt 3:16-17)

The Power of God's Voice

In Genesis 1, God spoke to create the universe and bring forth life. In Genesis 1:3, God said: "Light be." Light came forth. Light still obeys God's voice.

> For He spoke, and it was. He commanded, and it stood fast. (Ps 33:9)

And God continues to uphold (*sustain, preserve, and govern*) everything by His powerful Word. (Heb 1:3)

God's loving and gracious nature is revealed

The Scriptures show God through many name-titles, pictures, illustrations, mighty acts, and kind, loving deeds.

God spoke to Moses as a man speaks to his friend. When Moses asked to see God's glory, God proclaimed: "the LORD God is merciful and gracious, long-suffering, and abounding in goodness and truth . . ." (Ex 34:6).

King David wrote thousands of songs to and about the Lord. He announced: "The Lord is good to all, and His tender mercies are over all His works" (Ps 145:9).

So, through and through, the God-breathed Scriptures shine the light on God. They show His everlasting love, mercy, and grace. And they speak life to people in every generation.

God tells us the future

Historians write accounts of past human history. But God publishes man's history—in advance. He tells us what is going to happen hundreds, even thousands, of years ahead of time. No human or man-made machine can do such a marvelous thing!

More than 300 scriptures foretell the incarnation, life, crucifixion, resurrection, and ascension of Jesus the Messiah, the Savior, the Son of God.

The book of Revelation unveils the Lord Jesus, as He *is*, as He *was*, and as He *shall be forever* in majesty, glory, and power. And this prophecy details end of the age events and things to come thereafter.

Revelation presents the fantastic future in store for believers, but the terrible doom awaiting the devil and all those who reject Christ, God's gift of salvation to the world. Christ rejectors have no excuse. "For the grace of God that brings salvation has appeared to all." (Tit 2:11)

Receive the Book of Revelation blessing

> God blesses the one who reads the words of this prophecy to the church, and he blesses all who listen to its message and obey what it says, for the time is near. (Rev 1:3, NLT)

The whole book of Revelation is a prophecy—both a foretelling and a forthtelling. It concerns things which *must shortly come to pass*. God revealed it to the Lord Jesus, who by His angel showed it to John, who wrote it down for Christ believers in every age. (Rev 1:1)

God promises the one reading the prophecy is blessed. And the hearers who keep the prophecy are blessed. So, read it out loud, again and again, and be doubly blessed.

The purpose of God's revelation is manifold

The purpose of God's revelation through the Scriptures is so we:

1. can personally know and worship the only true God,
2. believe that Jesus is the Christ (the Messiah, the Anointed One), the Son of God, and
3. in believing can be assured we have everlasting life in His name. (Mt 16:16-19; Jn 20:31; 1 Jn 5:11-13)

And, through the Holy Scriptures, we can:

1. grow in grace and the knowledge of our Lord,
2. develop spiritual ears to know God's voice,
3. discover and do God's will,
4. develop strong faith in God to live in victory,
5. increasingly love God and one another.

And because God's living Word has the power to change everything, it to our advantage to find out everything God says in it.

God's Word is living and powerful

> For the word of God is living and powerful, and sharper than any two-edged sword, piercing even to the division of soul and spirit, and of joints and marrow, and is a discerner of the thoughts and intents of the heart. (Heb 4:12)

God's Word is *alive* with God-life! It is brimming full of miracle-working, life-giving, situation-changing power. Many books can stimulate one's mind. However, the Bible is the only book in the universe that can:

- lead to eternal salvation,
- set us free spirit, soul, and body,
- distinguish spirit from soul,
- critique the thoughts and intents of one's heart,
- renew and transform one's mind,
- heal, restore, deliver, and preserve
- infuse with God-life, God-light, God-truth, God-strength, and God-wisdom.

The Scriptures reveal God's will

The Holy Scriptures progressively reveal God's will. In the New Testament, two Greek words define God's will: *boulema* and *thelema*.

Boulema is the *sovereign, immutable, inevitable* will of God. These things will happen no matter what. Christ's second coming, God conforming believers to Christ's image, the judgment of the unrighteous, and a new heaven and new earth are examples.

Thelema, on the other hand, speaks of God's *desire, wish, pleasure*. When God expresses His will as a desire, our cooperation is needed.

For instance, God chose Paul to be an apostle. But He did not force Paul to accept this calling. Paul did so of his own free will. In Ephesians 1:1, Paul calls himself *an apostle of Jesus Christ by the will of God*.

Third John 1:2 says, "Beloved, I wish above all things that you may prosper and be in health, even as your soul prospers." While a customary greeting in John's day, this scripture also conveys God's overarching desire that we do well in life in every respect.

In keeping with His desire that we live victoriously, God has provided everything we need to do so. It is up to each of us to bring the will of heaven to bear in the earth—*as in heaven so in earth.* (Mt 6:10)

Say amen to God's promises

> For all the promises of God in Him are Yes, and in Him Amen, to the glory of God through us. (2 Cor 1:20)

In the New Testament, God has given us exceedingly great and precious promises. The yes to all these promises is in Christ. In, by, and through Him, we can say, "Amen." So be it.

Too often, we pray and ask God to give us something He has already given us in His Word. Instead, we should thank Him and receive by faith whatever His Word says we have.

Promises of Healing and Health

Seven hundred years before Messiah's death on the cross, the prophet Isaiah declared: "His stripes heal us." Looking back to the cross, the apostle Peter said Jesus' stripes healed us. (*See* Isa 53:5 and 1 Pet 2:24.)

Thus, healing is provided in Christ's work of redemption and is available to every believer.

And the same Holy Spirit who raised Christ from the dead dwells in every Christ believer. He can *revive, stimulate,* and *enliven* your mortal body. (Rom 8:11)

So, if you get sick, don't ask God to heal you. Rather: <u>Receive your healing</u>. <u>Command</u> sickness out of your body. <u>Declare</u>: "Father, your Word says Jesus' stripes healed me. Therefore, healing is mine according to Your Word. <u>Thank</u> You for healing me." (Mk 11:23; 1 Pet 2:24)

Promises of Divine Resources, etc.

Resources, privileges, protection, provision, power, and peace are within reach through the Holy Scriptures. Lay hold to all these things by faith. Have an unshakable confidence and trust in God and His Word.

Speak and act in agreement with what God has said. Through faith and cheerful persistence, we can possess what God promises. (Heb 6:12)

God's Word is forever

God's eternal Word stands firm in heaven. (Ps 119:89) Thus, the Word will accomplish God's purpose.

> For as the rain comes down, and the snow from heaven, and do not return there, but water the earth, and make it bring forth and bud, that it may give seed to the sower and bread to the eater,
> So shall My word be that goes forth from My mouth; it shall not return to Me void, but it shall

accomplish what I please, and it shall prosper in the thing for which I sent it. (Isa 55:10-11)

Conclusion: God's Word is priceless, profitable, reliable, and timeless

The Word of God is *priceless* because God gave us this amazing life-changing revelation free of charge.

God's Word is *profitable* because it will teach us the truth, convict our hearts of sin, correct our faults, and train us to live right. It will prepare and equip us for every good work. And it provides all the tools we need to *fight the good fight of faith* and be wonderfully victorious. (1 Tim 6:12)

God's Word is utterly *reliable* because God cannot lie. Whatever God says, you can count on it. (Heb 6:18; Num 23:19)

God's Word is *timeless*. It is as relevant today as it was when spoken thousands of years ago.

> The counsel of the Lord stands forever, the plans of His heart to all generations. (Ps 33:11)

Let us rejoice. We are recipients of a miraculous living book, breathed out by God Himself. We have evidence of God's everlasting love, credibility, and faithfulness.

***

May you increase more and more in hearing God's voice and living by grace through faith in His eternal Word.

2
JESUS CHRIST

> And this is eternal life, that they may know You, the only true God, and Jesus Christ whom You have sent. (Jn 17:3)

Here, we will look at the essence of God's Son. We will see how the Son connects us with the Father and how the Father speaks to us through the Son.

The Personal Word of God

The apostle John is the only gospel writer who begins his account of the life of Jesus with eternity. Right away, John introduces us to the eternal Word of God.

> In the beginning was the Word, and the Word was with God, and the Word was God. ² He was in the beginning with God. ³ All things were made through Him, and without Him nothing was made that was made. (Jn 1:1-3)

In the beginning was the Lógos, and the Lógos was *face-to-face* with God, and the Lógos was God. He was always in the eternal realm with God. Everything came into existence through Him.

In the Greek language, lógos means *expression of thought*. It is something said—*a word, statement, speech, divine utterance, message.*

John reveals that the Lógos, who was at the beginning with God, is, in fact, Jesus Christ, the Son of God. Christ tells out Deity, not in parts of speech as a sentence composed of words, but **personally through His life.**

> Eternal life is in Him, and this life gives light to all mankind. (Jn 1:4)

The Incarnation of the Word

So, around 4 AD, something super-amazing happened. The Son of God, the eternal Lógos of God, became flesh.

> The Word became flesh and lived among us. We gazed on his glory, the kind of glory that belongs to the Father's uniquely existing Son, who is full of grace and truth. (Jn 1:14, ISV)

The Word came to earth in the form of a babe through the womb of the Virgin Mary. He would be known as Jesus of Nazareth and called Immanuel, *with us, God.*

From the earth's standpoint, a virgin supernaturally conceived and bore a son. From Heaven's perspective, God gave us His Son, called *Wonderful, Counselor, Mighty God, Everlasting Father, Prince of Peace.* He is the eternal Word who became flesh. (Isa 9:6-7)

Jesus is fully divine and a perfect, sinless human—all in one.

Life, light, love, grace, and truth find full expression in Him. Amazing! Phenomenal!

God sent His Son, the Lógos, to personally express divinity. Through words, actions, and mighty deeds, Christ shows us the true God.

Christ came for our benefit

Christ came from Heaven to earth to:

1. clarify God
2. fulfill the law and the prophets
3. take on human nature, but without sin
4. set us free from the works of the devil
5. pay the death penalty to redeem us
6. grant us access to God and His kingdom
7. give us a new spirit indwelt by God's Spirit
8. give us authority, power, and dominion over evil
9. bring God-life, God-light, God-love, God-grace, and God-truth to everyone, and
10. show us who we are and why we are living.

Indeed, Christ suffered and died on the cross for our sins. Six centuries before, Isaiah declared:

> Surely our diseases He did bear and our pains He carried; whereas we did esteem Him struck down, smitten by God and afflicted. But He was wounded and slain for our transgressions and rebellion. He was beaten to pieces and crushed because of our iniquities, perversity, and evil. The punishment for our peace and well-being was upon Him, and by His stripes and blows, we are

healed, thoroughly repaired, and made whole."
(Isa 53:4-5, my paraphrase)

Three days and nights after His crucifixion and burial in a tomb, God resurrected Jesus out from the dead.

After His resurrection, Jesus was seen alive by Mary Magdalene, Mary (the mother of James), the original apostles, and many others, as the Scriptures tell us. (Mk 16:9; Mt 28:1-9; Jn 20:19; Acts 1:3; 1 Cor 15:5-8)

Before He ascended, the Lord told His apostles that He had been given all authority in Heaven and earth. He charged his apostles to wait for the outpouring of the Holy Spirit and then go to all nations preaching the good news of salvation, teaching, baptizing, and making disciples in His Name. (Lk 24:49; Acts 1:4, 8; Mt 28:18-20)

Christ's finished His work of salvation for us

The Lord bridged the gap between God and man by removing the sin that separated us from a Holy God. With His blood, He entered the Most Holy Place in Heaven once for all time and secured our eternal redemption. (Heb 9:12)

Through Christ, we have redemption, the forgiveness of sins, right-standing with God, eternal life, 24/7 access to the Father, favor that surrounds like a shield, privileges, and resources. (Eph 1:7, 1:3; Ps 5:12, Rom 5:2)

And we have a High Priest who, though tempted in every way that we are, did not sin. Thus, He can sympathize with our weaknesses, while at the same time help us overcome. (Heb 4:15; Rom 8:34; Phil 4:13)

Now seated at the right hand of the Father in Heaven, the Lord is waiting for his enemies to be made his footstool. (Heb 1:3b; Heb 10:13)

In Christ we have total victory

In Christ, instead of death for us, there is life. Instead of slavery to sin, there is freedom from sin.

And Jesus overcame the world for us.

> I have told you this so that through me you may have peace. In the world you'll have trouble, but be courageous—I've overcome the world! (Jn 16:33, ISV)

In Jesus, we are overcomers:

> You are of God, little children, and have overcome them, because He who is in you is greater than he who is in the world. (1 Jn 4:4)

> Everyone who is a child of God has the power to win against the world. It is our faith that wins the victory against the world. (1 Jn 5:4, ICB)

The Greek word for *overcome* is also translated *victory*. The verb nikaō (nē-kä'-ō) means to *overcome, conquer, prevail, get the victory* (*carry off the victory, come off victorious*). Today we might say: beat, conquer, defeat, master, outdo, overpower, overthrow, prevail over, subdue, triumph over and win.

Christ conquered everything that conquered us—sin, sickness and disease, lack, the world systems, the flesh, the devil, and death. Thus, in Christ, we are *more than conquerors*! That is, we are super victors, decisively and overwhelmingly victorious. (Rom 8:37)

Jesus Christ is God's final Word

Christ is God's final Word concerning everything.

> God, who at various times and in various ways spoke in time past to the fathers by the prophets, has in these last days spoken to us by His Son, whom He has appointed heir of all things, through whom also He made the worlds. (Heb 1:1-2)

Christ is forever the most glorious God-man. He is the brightness (*outshining radiance*) of God's glory and the express image (*exact likeness*) of His person. (Heb 1:3) *For in Him dwells all the fullness of the Godhead bodily.* (Col 2:9)

Christ is coming again soon. He is coming for His bride, the church. (1 Thess 4:13-18; 1 Cor 15:51-58)

And, He will return to bring the wrath of God on the enemies of God. (Rev 19:11-12; 14:19; Rom 1:18; Isa 13:13)

In the meantime, the Lord gives <u>whoever</u> will receive Him the right and privilege to become children of God and live forever with Him. (Jn 3:16; Jn 1:12; Rom 10:9-10)

3
CONSCIENCE

> Holding the mystery of the faith with a pure conscience (1 Tim 3:9)

God created people three parts in one—spirit, soul, and body. Our spirit is the center of God's activity in our life.

And God put three unique sensors in our spirit to keep us conscious of Him and sensitive to His voice. Those sensors are conscience, intuition, and communion.

The conscience is the seat of one's moral consciousness. More specifically, it is a built-in sense to know right from wrong with an urging to do right. It is God's moral law written in our hearts.

God intended the conscience to instantly judge our thoughts concerning right and wrong, even if we do not know His written moral law.

> for when Gentiles, who do not have the law, by nature do the things in the law, these, although not having the law, are a law to themselves, who show the work of the law written in their hearts, their conscience also bearing witness, and

> between themselves, their thoughts accusing or else excusing them. (Rom 2:14-15)

Every person innately knows right from wrong. Your conscience will accuse you when you think and act on wrong thoughts.

Sin separates us from God. And sin will cause us to self-justify and overrule the voice of conscience.

So, conscience can only be relied upon after God cleanses it with the sinless blood of Jesus.

the Blood of Jesus cleanses one's conscience

The good news is that the moment we repent and receive Christ, the Holy Spirit reconnects us with God. And the sinless blood of Jesus cleanses us from all sin.

> How much more will the blood of Christ, who through the eternal Spirit offered Himself without spot to God, purge your conscience from dead works to serve the living God. (Heb 9:14)

If, after receiving Christ, we continue to do wrong and ignore the voice of conscience, we will lose sensitivity.

Eventually, if one continues to override this inner voice, he or she could wind up with a seared conscience, i.e., entirely insensitive to God's voice. Indeed, no one wants to end up like that.

So, here is how to maintain a clear conscience.

Five steps to keep a clear conscience

1. If you sin, quickly repent.

To repent is to turn away from sin and turn to face God. Confess your sins to Him. The Lord promises: "If we confess our sins, He is faithful and just to forgive us our sins and to cleanse us from all unrighteousness" (1 Jn 1:9).

2. Immediately receive God's forgiveness.

Realize when you sincerely repent, God forgives you. Receive God's mercy. And, forgive yourself.

3. Receive purification by faith.

Let us draw near with a true heart in full assurance of faith, having our hearts sprinkled from an evil conscience, and our bodies washed with pure water. (Heb 10:22)

4. Renew your mind on God's Word.

Do not be conformed to this world, but be transformed by the renewing of your mind, that you may prove what is that good and acceptable and perfect will of God. (Rom 12:2)

When we daily renew our minds on God's Word which is full of light, we will begin to see ourselves as God sees us in Christ.

This is the key to thinking and acting like God originally intended—full of God-inspired thoughts, creative ideas, sparkling life, and purpose.

> 5. *Live honorably and honestly.*
>
> I am speaking the truth as one in union with Christ, and my own conscience, enlightened by the Holy Spirit, assures me it is no lie. (Rom 9:1)

***

God speaks to you personally through your conscience. So, stay pure, listen to your conscience, and do what you know is right.

4
INTUITION

> But immediately, when Jesus perceived in His spirit that they reasoned thus within themselves, He said to them, "Why do you reason about these things in your hearts?" (Mk 2:8)

Intuition is a gift of knowingness

The omniscient God placed a sense of knowing inside our spirit called intuition. It is one's internal perceiver or knower. Like conscience, intuition is part of our God-consciousness.

You may have said or heard someone say, "Something told me I should do this or that." Or "I just know deep down inside." We all have an inner knowingness that operates independent of rational thinking or reasoning.

Jesus demonstrates intuition

There are many instances where Jesus followed his intuition.

In Mark chapter 2, when people heard Jesus was in Capernaum, they came in swarms. Four men carrying a paralyzed man on a bed were unable to break through the crowd to get to Jesus. So, they went up on the roof of the house he was in, took the cover off, and let the man down on his bed. (Mk 2:3-4)

Seeing how much faith they had, Jesus said to the paralyzed man, "Son, your sins are forgiven." (2:5)

All the while, some of the scribes sitting there reasoned in their hearts, "Why does this man speak blasphemies like this? Who can forgive sins but God alone?" (2:6-7)

Immediately, Jesus perceived in his spirit what these men were thinking. He asked them, "Why do you reason about these things in your hearts?" (2:8a)

He then asked which was easier, to say to the paralytic, "Your sins are forgiven you," or to say, "Arise, take up your bed and walk?"

Jesus continued. "So that you may know the Son of Man has power on earth to forgive sins" – He said to the paralytic, "I say to you, arise, take up your bed, and go to your house." Immediately the man arose, took up his bed, and went his way. (2:8b-10)

Listen and respond to intuition

God intended this gift of knowingness to help us make the right decisions.

Of course, to maximize the effectiveness of intuition, one must be born again. With a new spirit rightly connected to God, we can more accurately discern the revelations of God and the movements of the Holy Spirit within.

Listening to your intuition is like having a quiet conversation with God. It might be an impression to pick up the phone and call a friend. Whenever I do, the person I call usually tells me my call is right on time. And our conversation often ends in mutual blessing.

There are times when responding immediately to intuition proves to be a matter of life or death.

Years ago, I was in a nightclub with my friend Linda. We were chatting and laughing when suddenly Linda said, "Something doesn't feel right. I think we should leave." So, we did. The next day, Linda called me. She said right after we left the club, someone came in and shot a lady sitting at a table near ours.

Other times, our intuition tells us to do something that will profoundly affect the future.

Jan, another friend, was impressed to speak to a man in the congregation that she hardly knew. Greg and Jan became fast friends, married, and have three lovely daughters.

More than a few people wished they had listened to their intuition when impressed to invest in the stock market but didn't. They reasoned they could not afford it at the time. However, had they followed their intuition and invested, by now, they would be wealthy.

Then, there are times when you are impressed to do some little thing that turns out to be a very big thing. Like adding something to your diet that you later find out is a tremendous health benefit.

This knowing in one's spirit is God's gift to help us make the right decisions in every dimension of life.

We sharpen this gift with use. The more we pay attention and respond to it, the more we will gain confidence that we indeed are hearing from God in a very unique and personal way.

Chapter 5

COMMUNION

> God is Spirit, and those who worship Him must worship in spirit and truth. (Jn 4:24)

Like conscience and intuition, communion is part of our God-consciousness. Specifically, communion calls us to worship and intimacy with God.

Communion, derived from com, *come together*, and union, *at one*, means a *blending together as one*.

When we are born again, God unites our spirit with His. Then, over time, as we have free-hearted, spontaneous communication with God, intimacy arrives.

Develop intimacy with God

After we are born again, it becomes clear we were born to worship God. Freshly aware of how God rescued us out of sin and all kinds of bondage, we have joy, peace, and lightness of being.

Singing to the Lord is what we do. Without a choir director, we make a joyful sound to the Lord. With child-like faith, we pray. We give thanks every time we think about God's goodness to us.

Soon, we find ourselves spending consecrated time in His presence. There are times of quiet reflection in His Word and listening to hear His voice when He speaks to our hearts.

As we continually delight ourselves in Him and endeavor to be sensitive to the inner promptings, leadings, and restraints of the Holy Spirit, communion with God results.

Psalm 91 exhorts us to live in the Secret Place

Psalm 91:1 says, "He who dwells in the secret place of the Most-High shall abide under the shadow of the Almighty."

This psalm speaks of finding safety and protection by dwelling in the secret place.

What is the secret place? Your heart. It is the private place where you and God commune, spirit to Spirit.

If you continually commune with God, you will live in divine safety and protection. And, there will be *defining moments* when your heart is so one with God that time disappears. You are one in the Spirit. Nothing else matters.

Take steps to live in the Secret Place

Be a full-time God-worshipper.

1. Sing and make melody in your heart to the Lord.

> Speak to each other with psalms, hymns, and spiritual songs. Sing and make music in your hearts to the Lord (Eph 5:19, ICB)

2. Pray and sing in the Spirit and with understanding.

   > So, here's what I've concluded. I will pray in the Spirit, but I will also pray with my mind engaged. I will sing rapturous praises in the Spirit, but I will also sing with my mind engaged. (1 Cor 14:15, TPT)

3. Pray for all people.

   > First of all, then, I urge you to offer to God petitions, prayers, intercessions and expressions of thanks for all people, for kings, and for everyone who has authority, so that we might lead a quiet and peaceful life with all godliness and dignity. (1 Tim 2:1-2, ISV)

4. Live in light and truth.

   > I have no greater joy than these things, that I hear my children are walking in truth. (3 Jn 1:4)

   > In the past you were full of darkness, but now you are full of light in the Lord. So, live like children who belong to the light. Light brings every kind of goodness, right living, and truth. (Eph 5:8-9, ICB)

   > But if we walk in the light as he is in the light, we have fellowship with one another, and the blood

of Jesus Christ His Son cleanses us from all sin. (1 Jn 1:7)

We were born to worship and commune with God. When we commune with Him, His heart of love becomes ours. We imitate Him. From there, we can change the world.

6
STILL SMALL VOICE

> Then He said, "Go out, and stand on the mountain before the Lord." And behold, the Lord passed by, and a great and strong wind tore into the mountains and broke the rocks in pieces before the Lord, but the Lord was not in the wind; and after the wind an earthquake, but the Lord was not in the earthquake; and after the earthquake a fire, but the Lord was not in the fire; and after the fire a still small voice. (1 Ki 19:11-12)

The above text carries the only reference in Scripture to a still small voice. The revelation of it, however, is powerful. But it may not be what you think. So, let's take a closer look.

Here is the still small voice backstory

By the 9th century B.C., Israel had become a nation of idol worshippers due in large part to its increasingly wicked leaders. King Ahab and his murderous wife, Queen Jezebel, were the worst.

Jezebel promoted the worship of false gods. She had 450 prophets of Baal and 400 prophets of Asherah for whom she provided. And, she hunted and killed as many of God's faithful prophets as she could find.

Elijah (*my God is Yahweh*) wanted to see Israel return to the Lord. He called for a god contest, if you will, on Mount Carmel, to demonstrate that Yahweh is God.

From morning to evening, the prophets of Baal called on Baal to send fire from heaven upon their altar. No response.

Elijah mocked them, after which he built the altar of the Lord. After that, he took four large jars of water and drenched the altar, the burnt sacrifice, and the wood three times. Then he prayed for God to send fire from heaven to consume the sacrifice.

The Lord sent fire. The fire consumed the sacrifice, wood, stones, dust, and all the water. The children of Israel fell on their faces and said, "The LORD, He is God. The LORD, He is God." (*See* 1 Ki 18:17-39)

After this supernatural display, Elijah executed the 450 prophets of Baal. (1 Ki 18:40) When Queen Jezebel learned of it, she sent a messenger to Elijah vowing to kill him in 24 hours.

Elijah fled Jezreel and went to Beersheba in Judah (about 95 miles). He left his servant in Beersheba and went a day's journey into the wilderness. Tired, thirsty, hungry, and discouraged, Elijah sat down under a broom tree and prayed to die. (1 Ki 19:3-4)

Elijah hears God speak

God sent an angel to provide Elijah with food and water. Elijah then traveled 40 days and nights until he came to Horeb (Mt. Sinai), where he went into the cave and spent the night. (1 Ki 19:7-9a)

Then the word of the Lord came to him, "What are you doing here, Elijah?" (1 Ki 19:9b). Notice, when Elijah got out of the panic mode, when he was still, Elijah could hear God's voice.

Without answering God's question, Elijah said, "God, everybody has forsaken your covenant. All the prophets are dead. I alone am left. Now they are trying to kill me, too." (v. 10, my paraphrase)

God said to Elijah: "Go out on the mountain and stand in the presence of the Lord. For, the Lord is about to pass by."

A fierce wind tore into the mountain and broke the rocks in pieces. Then there was an earthquake. After the earthquake, there was a fire. But the Lord was not in the fierce wind, earthquake, or fire. After the fire, a still small voice (vv. 11-12).

So, what was the *still small voice*? Sheer silence!

The atmosphere was *quiet, calm, still.* Then, Elijah wrapped his face in his mantle and went and stood in the entrance of the cave, where he waited for God to speak. Suddenly a voice came to him and said, "Elijah, what are you doing here?" (v. 13)

When Elijah stood quietly in the presence of the Lord, when God had his undivided attention, then God spoke and gave Elijah a clear perspective, fresh revelation, and new direction.

The *still small voice* is the atmosphere of God's presence

The still small voice then is not so much a way God speaks to us as it is the atmosphere in which He speaks.

I have found that often after a time of complete surrender and worshipping the Lord, a holy hush ensues. Sheer silence!

Then God's glory fills the atmosphere. Suddenly, God speaks. Refreshing words, new songs, fresh direction come from the presence of the Lord.

7
HOLY SPIRIT, THE ANOINTING WITHIN

> You have an anointing from the Holy One and know all things. (1 Jn 2:20)
>
> Now we have not received the spirit of the world, but the Spirit, who is from God, that we might know the things that are freely given to us from God. (1 Cor 2:12)

Today, there are masterclasses for everything. People want you to pay them enormous sums of money in exchange for some secret information on how to do this or that to be successful.

But, did you know, if you are born again, the Master Teacher lives in you? The Holy Spirit, the eternal Spirit of Truth, is the divine presence in every believer. His infinite knowledge, understanding, wisdom, and truth are priceless and without price.

What is the anointing?

The word *anointing* comes from the Greek *chrio*, which means *to smear or rub with oil, to consecrate*.

Under the Old Covenant, an oil was specially prepared to consecrate individuals God selected to stand in the office of prophet, priest, or king. The oil represented the Holy Spirit.

The Holy Spirit is the anointing

In the New Covenant, the Holy Spirit is the anointing. He is the agent of spiritual rebirth and dwells within the spirit of every Christ believer.

> The anointing you received from God abides in you, and you do not need anyone to teach you this. Instead, because God's anointing teaches you about everything and is true and not a lie, abide in him, as he taught you to do. (1 Jn 2:27, ISV)

So, because the Spirit of God lives within, you do not need anyone to teach you the truth. You know truth by the Spirit.

The Holy Spirit bears witness

The Holy Spirit bears witness with our spirit that we are God's children. "He who believes in the Son of God has the witness in himself." (1 Jn 5:10) Thus, the Holy Spirit is tangible assurance of eternal life.

The Holy Spirit is your Illuminator

The Holy Spirit is the Spirit of wisdom and revelation. He illuminates our heart and reveals treasures of knowledge and wisdom so we can live in the highest dimension of life rooted in Christ. (Eph 1:17-18)

The Spirit will teach us how to live by faith through God's grace. He will help us distinguish truth from error. Knowing and adhering to pure truth will keep us free from lies and deception.

The Holy Spirit is your Inside Informer

As your Inside Informer, the Holy Spirit speaks what He hears in the throne room of Heaven. When He speaks to your heart, He is sending you an instant message. It is a fresh word from the very heart of God our Father and the Lord Jesus Christ.

> For He will not speak on His own authority, but whatever He hears He will speak. (Jn 16:13b)

To me, the omniscient Spirit inside is like having an eternal living database where we can access and download wisdom and truth anytime day or night.

God says, "Call to Me, and I will answer you, and show you great and mighty things, which you do not know" (Jere 33:3).

The Lord will show and explain things to you that are inaccessible, unattainable, too lofty to know apart from God's revelation.

> As it is written, "No eye has seen, no ear has heard, and no mind has imagined the things that God has prepared for those who love him." But God has revealed those things to us by his Spirit. For the Spirit searches everything, even the deep things of God. (1 Cor 2:9-10, ISV)

Sometimes we feel the Spirit moving

Where the Spirit of the Lord is, there is always life, liberty, and movement.

At creation, the Spirit of God was moving, working with the Lord to bring light, life, and order to the dark and chaotic world. In the New Testament, the Spirit came upon Jesus' disciples as a *rushing, mighty wind.* (Acts 2:4)

Sometimes the Spirit moves in us softly. Other times, we may experience sensations inside and out.

On occasion, I have felt a quivering in my spirit as a witness to something significant taking place in the spirit realm. Sometimes after a season of fasting and intense prayer, I experienced this inner shaking.

A few times, my insides shook when I heard powerfully anointed preaching and teaching in conferences and church meetings.

One time I attended a conference where a certain speaker was called on to pray. The moment he said "Dear God," an anointing fell in that place. I felt a shaking in my spirit. The Holy Spirit bore witness with my spirit that God was very present in and among His people, and the things spoken were right.

The Spirit gives signs in one's spirit

The Holy Spirit gives us signs or signals in our spirit. A discordant note in one's inner man is like a red flag, a stoplight, a do-not-proceed indicator. Indeed, any time you do not sense God's life on something, continue no further.

Stay sensitive to the Holy Spirit

Every believer has the eternal Spirit of God dwelling within.

The Spirit is the divine revelator and illuminator of the divine. He will bear witness with your spirit to the truth of God's miraculous Word. So "let the word of God dwell richly in you in all wisdom" (Col 3:16).

Understand that the Holy Spirit always works with and according to the Holy Scriptures. Thus, when something is of God, the Spirit and the Word agree.

Always be aware of and sensitive to the revelation, witness, voice, wooing, leading, and restraint of God's Spirit within.

Keep on being filled with the Spirit

Ephesians 5:18 commands us not to be drunk with wine which leads to riotous living, but to stay full of the Spirit.

> Do not be drunk with wine. That will ruin you spiritually. But be filled with the Spirit. (Eph 5:18, ICB)

Another translation says:

> Be constantly, consciously, definitely, subjected to the Spirit, a life that has a consuming desire for His control over every thought, word, and deed; thus, a life unceasingly controlled by the Spirit. (Wuest, Vol 3, p. 110)

The Holy Spirit is a continual fountain of life to the inner man. Proverbs 18:14 says a person's spirit will sustain him in sickness. So, to have a strong spirit that will sustain you through sickness (and any other challenging thing), always, moment by moment, keep being filled and directed by the Holy Spirit.

Let the Spirit lead you in thought, word, and deed. He will guide you into all truth. And He works in you both to will and to do of God's good pleasure. (Jn 16:13; Phil 2:13)

8

AUDIBLE VOICE OF THE LORD

> For God may speak in one way, or in another, yet man does not perceive it. (Job 33:14)

The Lord's voice may sound like someone nearby talking to you. Or, His voice might be audible within. We will look at instances of both.

The child Samuel heard the audible voice of the Lord

As a child, Samuel quickly came to know the Lord's voice. You may recall that after weaning Samuel, Hannah took him to Eli, the priest, for Eli to train him for the priesthood.

One night while sleeping, Samuel awoke to the sound of someone calling his name. He thought Eli called him because no one else was there. Samuel got up and went to Eli's bed. But Eli told Samuel he did not call him.

Samuel went back to bed. Again, he heard someone calling him. Samuel went to Eli, and, once again, Eli told Samuel he did not call him.

Samuel returned to his bed. The voice called him a third time. This time Eli perceived the Lord was calling Samuel. So, Eli told Samuel to go lie down, and if someone called him again, to respond by saying, "Speak, Lord, for your servant hears" (1 Sam 3:9).

> Now the Lord came and stood and called as at other times, "Samuel, Samuel!" And Samuel answered, "Speak, for Your servant hears." (1 Sam 3:10)

Here, the Lord appeared and spoke to Samuel in a vision. (1 Sam 3:15)

The Apostle Peter while in a trance heard the audible voice of the Lord

An angel appeared in a vision to a devout soldier named Cornelius and told him to send for Peter. Around noon the next day, as Cornelius' messengers were nearing the seaport of Joppa to find Peter, Peter went up on the roof to pray.

> He was hungry and wanted to eat, but while lunch was being prepared, he fell into a trance and entered into another realm. As the heavenly realm opened up, he saw something resembling a large linen tablecloth that descended from above, being let down to the earth by its four corners. As it floated down, he saw that it held many kinds of four-footed animals, reptiles, and wild birds.

> A voice said to him, "Peter, go and prepare them to be eaten."
>
> Peter replied, "There's no way I could do that, Lord, for I've never eaten anything forbidden or impure *according to our Jewish laws*." (Acts 10:10-14, TPT)

Here, Peter was in a trance. He saw heaven open. A voice came to him. Peter recognized the Lord's voice. It took him a while to get God's message, but he finally got it. The gospel of salvation was for all people, not just the Jews.

Of note, about eight centuries earlier, the prophet Jonah was sent from Joppa to deliver God's message to Nineveh, the capital of the Assyrian Empire. "Yet forty days and Nineveh shall be overthrown." (Jonah 3:4)

The Assyrians repented, fasted, and cried out to God. So, with great mercy, God stayed judgment.

Saul of Tarsus encountered the resurrected Lord Jesus and heard His voice

Saul of Tarsus was on his way to Damascus with letters from the high priest in Jerusalem, authorizing Saul to arrest followers of Christ. Suddenly, he spectacularly encountered the resurrected Lord Jesus.

> Just outside the city, a brilliant light flashing from heaven suddenly exploded all around him. Falling to the ground, he heard a booming voice

say to him, "Saul, Saul, why are you persecuting me?"

The men accompanying Saul were stunned and speechless, for they heard a heavenly voice but could see no one.

Saul replied, "Who are you, Lord?"

"I am Jesus, the Victorious, the one you are persecuting. Now, get up and go into the city, where you will be told what you are to do."

Saul stood to his feet, and even though his eyes were open he could see nothing—he was blind. So, the men had to take him by the hand and lead him into Damascus. For three days he didn't eat or drink and couldn't see a thing. (Acts 9:3-9, TPT)

Saul's encounter with the Lord and conversion is so significant it is recorded three times in Acts (chapters 9, 22, and 26). Saul became known by Paul, his Latin name.

The Lord may speak today in an audible voice

The Lord has spoken to me three times in an audible voice. One time I was in a nightclub. I heard a clear, distinct voice inside me: "What are you doing in this den of iniquity?" I left and never went back. Then I rededicated my life to the Lord and began the greatest adventure of my life with Him.

God knows what it takes to get each of us going in the right direction. And, if He so chooses, He may speak to you in an audible voice.

9
FRUIT OF SPIRIT

> But the fruit produced by the Holy Spirit within you is divine love in all its varied expressions: joy that overflows, peace that subdues, patience that endures, kindness in action, a life full of virtue, faith that prevails, gentleness of heart, and strength of spirit. Never set the law above these qualities, for they are meant to be limitless. (Gal 5:22-23, TPT)

The Holy Spirit works in the heart of a believer to produce godly character. The core of that character is love.

God is Love

God is love. The kind of love that God is by nature is called agapē (ag-ah'-pay). Agapē is a pure, spontaneous, unconditional, tenaciously devoted love. It is a love that always gives and seeks the highest good for the recipient.

Go where God's love leads

One time I was jogging along Wilshire Boulevard near Beverly Hills when a man got my attention by crying out, "Lady, do you have a dollar?" I turned to look at him, apologizing that I didn't have any money with me.

As I continued to run, an overwhelming sense of compassion engulfed me. I began to shake. The look of sadness in that man's eyes kept flashing in my mind, over and over.

After I got home and showered, I knew I had to go back to the Boulevard to find that man. I felt impressed to give him some money, but, more importantly, to tell him that the finger of God, so to speak, was pointing at him, because God was not going to let me rest until I responded to the man's need.

At first, I didn't see him as I drove up and down Wilshire Boulevard. Then, I spotted him sitting at a bus stop, with his head down. He looked so utterly hopeless, sad, and defeated.

As I locked my car and began to walk in his direction, a bus stopped, and he got on. I took a moment to be still and listen to my inner self. If ever I was sure of anything, I knew I was supposed to follow the bus and connect with the man when he got off. So, I got back into my car and followed the bus.

Each time the bus stopped, I waited expectantly to see if he would get off. At one point, thoughts went through my mind of how utterly foolish this was following a bus to God knows where to meet a total stranger who might be a serial killer.

At last, the bus stopped at the intersection of 7th and Hope Streets in downtown Los Angeles, and the man got off. I quickly pulled over to the curb behind the bus and honked to get his attention. He bent down to peer at me through the windshield, looking somewhat perplexed. Nevertheless, he waited for me to park and get out of the car.

As we stood face to face, I told him the Lord sent me after him. I handed him a $20 bill. You would have thought I had given him a million dollars. He looked at me in amazement and said, "Lord, have mercy!" I told him that was surely right; he was a treasure to God.

About this time, he reached out to hug me with tears streaming down his face. There we were, in the middle of the street, strangers, embracing like long-lost relatives.

God expanded my horizons that day. He gave me a glimpse beyond the limits of my objective reasoning into the dimension of His unconditional love. As I drove away, love filled my heart. Joy clapped its hands. Peace enveloped me.

Joy and peace are signs of God's presence

Joy can be a calm delight, a quiet sense of well-being, a sense of triumph, or exuberant gladness. The God kind of peace is a supernatural calm, tranquility, or harmony. One is untroubled, of undisturbed composure.

God spoke to the Jews as they were leaving Babylon, where they had been in captivity 70 years:

> For you will leave your exile with joy and be led home wrapped in peace. The mountains and hills in front of you will burst into singing and the trees of the field will applaud! (Isa 55:12, TPT)

For Christ believers, the Holy Spirit leads us out of the bondage of sin into God's kingdom of *righteousness, and peace, and joy in the Holy Spirit* (Rom 14:17).

God imputes Christ's righteousness to us. "Christ had no sin. But God made him become sin. God did this for us so that, in Christ, we could become right with God." (2 Cor 5:21, ICB)

The result is immediate peace with God and, ergo, the supernatural peace of God, which supersedes natural understanding.

Isaiah wrote, "The work of righteousness is peace; and the result of righteousness is quietness and confidence forever." (Isa 32:17. TPT)

Joy and peace can be a green light

Together, joy and peace can provide a green light to proceed in a specific direction. But a green light does not always mean to "go" right now. God might not fulfill that word until years in the future.

So, when you get a personal word from the Lord, pray over it. Plan for it and work toward it. But wait on God's timing.

10

WORD OF WISDOM

> [7] But the manifestation of the Spirit is given to each one for the profit of all: [8] for to one is given the word of wisdom through the Spirit . . . [11] But one and the same Spirit works all these things, distributing to each one individually as He wills. (1 Cor 12:7-8, 11)

God might speak to a corporate body or an individual through manifestations of the Holy Spirit.

What is a manifestation of the Spirit?

A manifestation of the Spirit is an *outshining* of the Holy Spirit in a supernatural disclosure, expression, or exhibition.

The Holy Spirit works through the faith of people He chooses to bring to light, express, or exhibit part of the infinite wisdom, knowledge, glory, love, and power of God, as revealed in the Holy Scriptures.

These expressions and exhibitions are supernatural, spontaneous, and often spectacular. They benefit a person or persons needing a revelation, inspiration, or miraculous work at a given time.

There are nine manifestations revealed in 1 Corinthians 12. For our purposes, we will look at the three revelatory disclosures—a word of wisdom, a word of knowledge, and discerning of spirits. Here, we will look at a word of wisdom.

What is a word of wisdom?

A word of wisdom is a supernaturally imparted fragment of God's wisdom fitting for the occasion given by the Holy Spirit to or through a cooperating believer. (Isa 11:2)

The Holy Spirit gives a word of wisdom so that a person or people might have the right word at the right time to move forward in God's plan.

Joshua received war strategies

Joshua received God's wisdom to march around the city of Jericho once a day for six days and then seven times on the seventh day. On the seventh day, seven priests blew trumpets. Then Joshua told the people to "Shout, for the Lord has given you the city!" When the people shouted, the wall to the city fell flat. (*See* Joshua 6.)

Later, Joshua received a word of wisdom to command the sun to stand still.

> "Do not be afraid of them," the Lord said to Joshua, "for I have given you victory over them.

> Not a single one of them will be able to stand up to you. (Josh 10:8, NLT)
>
> On the day the Lord gave the Israelites victory over the Amorites, Joshua prayed to the Lord in front of all the people of Israel. He said,
>
> "Let the sun stand still over Gibeon and the moon over the valley of Aijalon." (Josh 10:12, NLT)

The result:

> So, the sun stood still and the moon stayed in place until the nation of Israel had defeated its enemies. (Josh 10:13, NLT)

Jesus promised divinely imparted wisdom to believers

> And remember this: When people accuse you before everyone and forcefully drag you before the religious leaders and authorities, do not be troubled. Don't worry about defending yourself or be concerned about how to answer their accusations. Simply be confident and allow the Spirit of Wisdom access to your heart, and he will reveal in that very moment what you are to say to them." (Luke 12:11-12, TPT)

How is the word of wisdom delivered?

A word of wisdom from God might be spoken out in prophecy, given through supernaturally inspired language with its interpretation, provided through a dream or vision, or come through the audible voice of the Lord.

***

God is ever-present in the person of the Holy Spirit. Trust Him to help you say and do the right thing in all areas of your life. And trust Him to manifest to you personally and through you corporately if He so chooses to help us all move forward in God's plan.

11

WORD OF KNOWLEDGE

> ⁷ But the manifestation of the Spirit is given to each one for the profit of all: ⁸ for to one is given the word of wisdom through the Spirit, to another the word of knowledge through the same Spirit... ¹¹ But one and the same Spirit works all these things, distributing to each one individually as He wills. (1 Cor 12:7-8, 11)

What is a word of knowledge?

A word of knowledge is not intellectually acquired. It is not mind reading or fortune-telling.

A word of knowledge is a fragment of divine knowledge supernaturally given by the omniscient Holy Spirit. It is a revelation about persons, places, or things in the present or past.

What is the setting for a word of knowledge?

We typically think of the manifestations of the Holy Spirit in the context of church assemblies. Years ago, I discovered that the Holy Spirit would reveal, exhibit, or express supernatural workings whenever and wherever

He chooses. I receive words of knowledge often during or after intercessory prayer.

Realize the Holy Spirit might give you a word of knowledge concerning a person for whom you are praying. Or, in any situation, public or private.

A blind prophet knows who is at the door

In 1 Kings 14, the Lord gives the blind prophet Ahijah a word of knowledge.

> Now the Lord had said to Ahijah, "Here is the wife of Jeroboam, coming to ask you something about her son, for he is sick. Thus, and thus you shall say to her; for it will be, when she comes in, that she will pretend to be another woman."
>
> And, so it was, when Ahijah heard the sound of her footsteps as she came through the door, he said, "Come in, wife of Jeroboam. Why do you pretend to be another person? For I have been sent to you with bad news." (1 Ki 14:4-6)

Jesus read the Samaritan woman's mail

In the story of the Lord's encounter with the Samaritan woman, at one point, he told her to get her husband. The woman said she did not have a husband.

Jesus responded that the woman had rightly spoken because she had been married five times, and the man with whom she was then living was not her husband. The woman said she perceived Jesus was a prophet since he knew these things about her. (Jn 4:16-19)

In His earthly ministry, Jesus operated as a prophet anointed by the Holy Spirit. Acts 10:38 says, "God anointed Jesus of Nazareth with the Holy Spirit and with power, who went about doing good and healing all who were oppressed by the devil, for God was with Him."

The Holy Spirit often manifests words of knowledge, words of wisdom, and prophetic words through God's prophets.

Peter knew Ananias and Sapphira lied

> A certain man named Ananias, with Sapphira his wife, sold a possession. And he kept back part of the proceeds, his wife also being aware of it, and brought a certain part and laid it at the apostles' feet. But Peter said, "Ananias, why has Satan filled your heart to lie to the Holy Spirit and keep back part of the price of the land for yourself? While it remained, was it not your own? And after it was sold, was it not in your own control? Why have you conceived this thing in your heart? You have not lied to men but to God. (Acts 5:1-4)

The backdrop to this story is that the multitude of believers in the early church was of one heart and soul and had all things in common. They sold their houses, land, and other possessions and brought the proceeds to the apostles to distribute as people had need.

Ananias and his wife sold property and retained some of the funds for themselves. There was no sin in that. The crime was one of pretense. They lied about the selling price to appear more pious and generous than they were. God considered their lying to the apostles the same as lying to Him.

Paul was forbidden to go to Asia

> Now when they had gone through Phrygia and the region of Galatia, they were forbidden by the Holy Spirit to preach the word in Asia. After they had come to Mysia, they tried to go into Bithynia, but the Spirit did not permit them. So, passing by Mysia, they came down to Troas. (Acts 16:6-8)

It was crucial that Paul heard and obeyed the restraints of the Holy Spirit here. The next verse explains why:

> And a vision appeared to Paul in the night. A man of Macedonia stood and pleaded with him, saying, "Come over to Macedonia and help us." Now after he had seen the vision, immediately we sought to go to Macedonia, concluding that the Lord had called us to preach the gospel to them. (Acts 16:9-10)

While Paul was in Troas on his second missionary journey, he had a vision that a man from Macedonia pled with him to come to Macedonia to help them. If Paul had gone to Asia, he would have missed God's plan for Macedonia.

Paul experienced great ministry in Macedonia

Paul's first stop in Macedonia was Philippi. On the Sabbath, he went out to the riverside. A group of women customarily prayed there. Among them was Lydia, a seller of purple from the city of Thyatira.

Lydia believed in and worshipped God. After Paul expounded the Scriptures, he baptized Lydia and her household. Lydia then persuaded Paul and Silas to stay at her house.

Later, officers arrested Paul and Silas for casting out a spirit of divination (fortune-telling) from a slave girl. At midnight Paul and Silas were praying and singing hymns to God. The prisoners were listening. Suddenly there was an earthquake. The foundations of the prison shook, the doors opened, and everyone's chains fell off.

The jailer who had fallen asleep was going to kill himself, thinking the prisoners had escaped under his watch. Paul assured him everyone was still there. Afterward, the jailer and his family received Christ.

Paul later spent three months in Corinth. He wrote Second Corinthians and also Romans. If Paul had not gone to Macedonia when he did, he might have delayed or aborted writing these letters which are a tremendous gift to the whole world.

How does a word of knowledge come?

Paul's word of knowledge came through a vision. A word of knowledge might also be spoken out in prophecy, given through supernaturally inspired language with its interpretation, or come through the audible voice of the Lord.

Word of Knowledge

Words of wisdom and words of knowledge often accompany the five-fold ministry gifts. They should also come through believers today, as the Holy Spirit wills.

12

DISCERNING OF SPIRITS

> ⁷ But the manifestation of the Spirit is given to each one for the profit of all ... ¹⁰ to another the working of miracles, to another prophecy, to another discerning of spirits ... ¹¹ But one and the same Spirit works all these things, distributing to each one individually as He wills. (1 Cor 12:7, 10, 11)

What is discerning of spirits?

Discerning of spirits is not extrasensory perception. It is a supernatural revelation from God as to the nature of a spirit. The purpose of discerning of spirits is to know whether those speaking into our lives are of God or not.

There are four kinds of spirits

The four kinds of spirits are:

>God
>Angels
>Humans
>Evil, demonic, or satanic spirits

God created angels and humans

God is the source of all life. He created angels in the dateless pass before He created humans. In fact, angels were there when God created the world.

> Where were you when I made the earth's foundation? Tell me, if you understand . . . Who did all this while the morning stars sang together? Who did this while the angels shouted with joy? (Job 38:4, 7 ICB)

Some angels rebelled against and became evil spirits

At some point, Lucifer rebelled against God, taking with him one-third of the angels. These fallen angels became a hierarchy of evil spirits under Satan. They operate in the lower heavens and atmosphere around us. And they work around the clock to influence and control humans. (Isa 14:12-17; Ezek 28:12-19; Rev 12:7-9; Eph 6:12)

When can evil spirits take control of a person?

The Spirit of God came upon King Saul whenever he was in the presence of the prophets. Saul prophesied and turned into a Spirit-anointed man.

But, back in his palace, Saul was willful, stubborn, and deeply jealous of David, who was God's choice to be Israel's next king. One time, Saul threw a spear at David. Saul eventually became so full of jealousy and rage that an evil spirit took control of him. (1 Sam 10:6; 16:14-23)

Jesus explains how evil spirits can take control and dominate a person's life:

> When an evil spirit comes out of a man, it travels through dry places looking for a place to rest. But it finds no place to rest.
>
> [44] So the spirit says, "I will go back to the home I left." When the spirit comes back to the man, the spirit finds the home still empty. The home is swept clean and made neat.
>
> [45] Then the evil spirit goes out and brings seven other spirits even more evil than it is. Then all the spirits go into the man and live there. And that man has even more trouble than he had before. It is the same way with the evil people who live today." (Mt 12:43-45, ICB)

An unclean spirit will return to a person not filled with God's spirit.

Strange phenomena in the atmosphere may point to the presence of evil spirits

As a child, I was aware of parallel worlds – the physical world I could see and another realm I could not see but knew existed.

I remember one house we lived in where the dog was always barking, especially at the door to the attic. One time we tried to open the attic door, but couldn't. The door locked from the inside. Later, the door opened, but no one was there.

On another occasion, I noticed the tall vase on the dining room table rocked back and forth, but the chandelier above it did not move at all. And the dog with hair standing up was all the while barking. Creepy, but stuff like this happened often.

It would come as no surprise in my later reflections that evil spirits had every right to live in that house—we were always taking in godless roomers with lots of issues and bad habits.

Physical reactions may point to presence of evil spirits

Sometimes I smell foul odors coming from people. It is not like the smell of someone who has not had a bath. Instead, it is putrid, like rotting flesh. I discovered this physical reaction alerted me to the presence of an unclean spirit in a person. Sort of like, "I smell a dead rat."

By the way, there are references in the Bible to all kinds of evil spirits (e.g., a lying spirit, a haughty spirit, the spirit of fear, the spirit of bondage, the spirit of heaviness, and seducing spirits). We recognize them by the characteristics they display through people.

However, Jesus made dealing with evil spirits simple. He called them all *unclean* and commanded them to go.

Sometimes we glimpse into the spirit realm

I have seen into the spirit realm many times, in dreams and open-eye visions. When I was in childbirth with my son, I saw the Lord. And I have seen angels as well as demonic spirits several times. (*See* Chapter 15, Prophetic Dreams and Visions).

Whatever our personal experiences, we must always test the spirits to see whether they are of God.

Test the spirits

> Dear friends, do not believe everyone who claims to speak by the Spirit. You must test them to see if the spirit they have comes from God. For there are many false prophets in the world. This is how we know if they have the Spirit of God: If a person claiming to be a prophet acknowledges that Jesus Christ came in a real body, that person has the Spirit of God. (1 Jn 4:1-2, NLT)

Do not believe every spirit, because the world is full of lies, liars, and lying wonders.

Test the spirit by the Word and the Holy Spirit.

- Does it line up with God's Word?
- Does it confess that Jesus Christ has come in the flesh?

The voice of antichrist is clear

> But if someone claims to be a prophet and does not acknowledge the truth about Jesus, that person is not from God. Such a person has the spirit of the Antichrist, which you heard is coming into the world and indeed is already here. (1 Jn 4:3, NLT)

A clear distinction between the people of the world and the people of God is found in their respective attitudes towards Jesus Christ. The world denies Him. We love and adore Him.

Undoubtedly, anyone who refuses to confess faith in Jesus is under the influence of the spirit of antichrist.

> These people belong to the Christ-denying world. They talk the world's language and the world eats it up. (1 Jn 4:5, Msg)

> We know that we are of God, and the whole world lies under the sway of the wicked one. (1 Jn 5:19)

The wicked one is the devil, called Satan. For a little while, he is the god of this present age.

The voice of God is clear

Every spirit (person, teacher, prophet, angel) that confesses that Jesus Christ has come in the flesh comes from God and belongs to God. These voices always witness to and glorify Jesus.

***

A spirit is behind every voice. The Holy Spirit will help us discern the spirit behind the voices who speak into our lives.

13

PROPHECY

> ⁷ But the manifestation of the Spirit is given to each one for the profit of all ... ¹⁰ to another the working of miracles, to another prophecy ... ¹¹ But one and the same Spirit works all these things, distributing to each one individually as He wills. (1 Cor 12:7, 10. 11)

There are three inspirational manifestations of the Holy Spirit. They are supernaturally inspired prophecy, different kinds of Holy Spirit inspired languages and the interpretation of the message given in those languages. Here, we will look at the manifestation of prophecy.

What is prophecy?

Prophecy primarily is *telling forth* the mind, heart, and will of God. About one-third of the Holy Scriptures *foretells* the future.

To prophesy is to speak or sing by divine inspiration in prediction or simple discourse.

The purpose of prophecy is to edify (*build up*), comfort (*cheer up*), exhort (*stir up*) the hearers. (1 Cor 14:3)

How is prophecy expressed?

In the New Testament prophecy is expressed four ways:

- through a prophet (Eph 4:11; 1 Cor 12:28)
- through one possessing a gift of prophecy (Rom 12:6)
- through any believer (Joel 2:28; Rev 19:10)
- through special manifestations of the Holy Spirit (1 Cor 12:10-11)

Prophets hear from God and under divine inspiration prophesy to comfort, encourage, warn, affirm, and strengthen God's people. (*See* Chapter 19, Ministry Gifts.)

A person endowed with a gift (*charisma*) of prophecy is graced with ongoing prophetic insight and forthright speaking.

Any believer can prophesy by faith under the anointing of the Holy Spirit. The testimony of Jesus Christ is the spirit of prophecy.

What distinguishes a special manifestation of prophecy?

A unique manifestation of prophecy is when the Holy Spirit chooses and prompts someone to speak forth an impromptu God-inspired message.

The selected speaker, compelled by the Spirit, opens his mouth and begins to speak as the Spirit gives him or her the words.

When the selected speaker cooperates with the Spirit, the result is divinely inspired communication in the language of the hearers that clearly expresses the immediate heart, mind, and will of God.

It is as though God, watching and listening, interrupts a service or event to give His real-time perspective!

I have experienced this often, both publicly and privately. While sometimes teaching from an outline, suddenly, the Holy Spirit prompts me to speak forth God's message in that instant.

Other times, I might be praying for someone when suddenly, God gives me prophetic words to speak into their lives.

In charismatic churches in the 1980s and 1990s, it was common for believers to stand up in a church service and prophesy by faith. Most times, they gave an encouraging message.

On occasion, there would be a *rumbling* in the spirit, like in Acts 2:2, when suddenly a sound came from heaven *like a mighty rushing wind*!

Sometimes, after dynamic heart-felt worship, prophecy poured forth powerfully. God's sweet presence filled the room like a thick cloud. People stood in awe, got on their knees, or lay prostrate in honor of Him.

These were moments that changed lives and greatly encouraged and strengthened believers. The Bible says we should earnestly desire the best gifts to be in operation – the one(s) most needed for the situation.

True Prophecy Syncs our Hearts with God's

True prophecy spoken under the inspiration of the Holy Spirit will:

1. Agree with Scripture (the more-sure prophetic word, 2 Pet 1:19)
2. Glorify the Lord Jesus Christ (Rev 19:10)
3. Be liberating and transformational (2 Cor 3:17)
4. Express divine love (1 Cor. 13:4-8)
5. Lift, build up, and stir up the hearers (1 Cor 14:3)
6. Be confirmed by two or three witnesses (2 Cor 13:1).
7. Bear witness with your spirit (Rom 8:16)
8. Draw people closer to God.

Inspired prophecy ushers us into a fresh alignment with the heart and purpose of God. With great enthusiasm, we advance His kingdom.

Test all Prophecies

> Beloved, do not believe every spirit, but test the spirits, whether they are of God; because many false prophets have gone out into the world. (1 Jn 4:1)

Hold all prophecies up to the light of the Scriptures.

Does the prophecy line us with the excellent nature and character of God? Does it exalt the Lord? A word from

God will not bring confusion or condemnation. And it will not contradict God's written Word.

Further, when you receive personal prophecies, always remember that other people are confirming voices only. They should not give you directives for your life. That is the Holy Spirit's job.

When you receive a personal prophecy, what should you do?

1. Please write it down, or get a recording, if available.
2. Test the prophecy by the Word and the Spirit, and prayer.
3. Keep a humble attitude and stay in faith.
4. Wait on God's timing.

Revisiting written prophecies or listening to a recording of them is an excellent way to encourage yourself during times of uncertainty – when it seems as though they will never come to pass.

When we receive prophecies, sometimes, our minds start racing. We try to figure out what, when, how, how long. Stop. Don't add your interpretation. Seek God's.

Test the prophecy by the Word. Per 2 Corinthians 13:1, establish every Word by two or three witnesses. Start by finding two or three scriptures that substantiate what you believe God is saying.

When will the prophecy be fulfilled?

Only God can tell you this.

David received prophecies that he would be king of Israel and Judah while he was a young boy taking care of his father's sheep. At the Lord's direction, the prophet Samuel secretly anointed the lad to be king.

However, it was a dozen or more years later, after much adversity, that David became king and reigned 40 years.

One thing I have learned about God, He moves according to His timetable, not ours. I like what Isaiah says:

> And therefore, the Lord [earnestly] waits [expecting, looking, and longing] to be gracious to you; and therefore, He lifts Himself up, that He may have mercy on you and show loving-kindness to you. For the Lord is a God of justice. Blessed (happy, fortunate, to be envied) are all those who [earnestly] wait for Him! (Isa 30:18, AMPC)

God waits that He may be more gracious. Wow!

Know that the Holy Spirit is ever-present and active to reveal God's will to you in personal and tangible ways and to encourage and strengthen you along the way. One of the tools He uses is a supernaturally inspired prophecy.

14

SPIRITUAL LANGUAGES AND INTERPRETATION

> [7] But the manifestation of the Spirit is given to each one for the profit of all ... [10] to another different kinds of tongues, to another the interpretation of tongues, [11] But one and the same Spirit works all these things, distributing to each one individually as He wills. (1 Cor 12:7, 10, 11)

Different kinds of tongues (*glossolalia*) or languages make up a Holy Spirit prompted and inspired message from God through a believer in a language he did not know or learn.

The Holy Spirit inspires the language and He gives the same speaker or someone else in the congregation the interpretation of the language.

Through the language and interpretation, God speaks to convey his heart at a precise moment to a person or group of people.

The tongue and tongues defined

The Greek *glossa* (*glossolalia,* plural) means (1) the tongue as an organ of speech; (2) tongues like as of fire which appeared at Pentecost; (3) a language; and (4) the supernatural speaking in another language not learned or acquired.

Believers speak in other languages

As promised, after the Lord's ascension, the Lord sent the Holy Spirit to about 120 Christ believers, including the apostles, the women, and Mary, the mother of Jesus.

Assembled in the upper room in Jerusalem, suddenly a sound came from heaven like *a mighty rushing wind.* Cloven tongues of fire sat on each of them. And they were all filled with the Holy Spirit and began to speak in languages they had not learned. (Acts 2:4)

Jews from every nation heard and understood their respective language. This phenomenon was a sign to unbelievers that God was present, and the gospel is for all people. (1 Cor 14:22; Acts 10:44-46)

Manifestation of different kinds of languages is still a sign to unbelievers

Different kinds of languages are still a miraculous sign to unbelievers. (1 Cor 14:22) They show unbelievers that God is watching and knows the secrets of their hearts.

I have been in meetings where God singled out and ministered to one person in the congregation through a stranger speaking a Holy Spirit inspired language that turned out to be that person's native language—some remote dialect.

In essence, the service stopped just for ministry to one person. That person became overwhelmed by God's amazing love and grace, which brought him or her to a place of heart conviction and repentance.

What is interpretation of different kinds of languages?

Interpretation of different kinds of languages is the supernatural ability of a believer inspired by the Holy Spirit to express the essential meaning of a message spoken in other tongues or languages.

The interpreter does not give a translation, as when an interpreter understands the language spoken. Instead, under the inspiration of the Holy Spirit, the interpreter declares the essential meaning of the message though he or she did not know the language. The interpretation is miraculous, supernatural.

Guidelines for corporate gathering

There are guidelines for the speaking in tongues in a corporate setting:

1. All things are to uplift (1 Cor 14:26);

2. All things are to be done decently and in order, that is, "in a gracious manner" (1 Cor 14:40); and

3. In a corporate setting, any Holy Spirit inspired language should be interpreted. (1 Cor 12:10, 14:5, 13, 15)

***

A Holy Spirit inspired language may minister to only one person. Yet, when someone gives the inspired interpretation, it is equal to prophecy for the rest of the congregation. Revelation, knowledge, and teaching are released. Everyone receives edification. (1 Cor 14:6)

15

PROPHETIC DREAMS AND VISIONS

> And it shall come to pass afterward, I will pour out My Spirit on all flesh; your sons and your daughters shall prophesy, your old men shall dream dreams, your young men shall see visions. (Joel 2:28)

Throughout the Bible, God spoke to His people through dreams and visions. This prophecy by Joel spoke of time *afterward* (*last days* in Isaiah 2:2) when God's Spirit would be poured out on all flesh, that is, on everyone who believes, Jew and Gentile.

This prophecy of an outpouring of God's Spirit began to be fulfilled several hundred years later on the Day of Pentecost A.D. 29 when the Spirit-filled church and the last days began. (Acts 2:16-21)

By many Scripture accounts, we are living in the last of the last days. Certainly, God continues to speak powerfully to His people through prophetic dreams and visions.

Dreams can be ordinary or extraordinary

Dreams are like watching movies while asleep. Some are rather ordinary. Others are supernatural and revelatory.

Outside stimuli can induce dreams. Ecclesiastes 5:3 says: "for a dream comes through much activity."

Demons can inspire dreams. Jeremiah 23:25-26 speaks of prophets who were deceived by their hearts.

Dreams inspired by God's Spirit are prophetic. They reveal something God wants us to know about ourselves, someone else, or some part of His plan and purpose. Thus, they may include a word of knowledge or a word of wisdom.

> For God may speak in one way, or in another, yet man does not perceive it. In a dream, in a vision of the night, when deep sleep falls upon men, while slumbering on their beds. Then He opens the ears of men, and seals their instruction. (Job 33:14-16)

The author of *Prophetic Dreams and Visions*, James Ryle, tells us six things God-inspired dreams do. They:

1. provide God's answers to our questions (as in Judges 7:10-15);
2. instruct us in the things of God (e.g. Mt 1:19-21);
3. warn us about unseen dangers (e.g. Mt 2:12, 13, 22);
4. guide us away from wrongdoing (e.g. Gen 20:3-8; 31:24; Mt 27:19);

5. keep us from pride (e.g. Dan 4:19-37); and
6. save our lives (e.g. Mt 2:13).

Might I add, God sometimes gives us dreams simply to encourage us.

One time while in Denver visiting a church with my son, I felt impressed to help an evangelist and his team by paying their hotel bill for that Sunday and Monday. The evangelist asked if I could take care of the hotel bill through Wednesday when they were leaving.

Yes, I had a moment of panic when I thought about how large my American Express bill was going to be. But I knew this was God's idea, not mine.

Back home in California, I had a dream. Suddenly a message appeared across the sky: "American Express, she was in Denver on my business." My dream ended with some angels cheering and applauding. Wow! Was that encouraging, or what? And, of course, God paid the bill.

Finally, if you have a dream you believe is from God, but you do not understand it, ask God for the interpretation. He is the One who gave it to you. And, remember, dreams from God will always line up with the Holy Scriptures.

Visions can occur while one is sleep or woke

Visions are like dreams, but often occur while one is awake. They are always supernatural and revelatory.

The Bible reveals three types of visions.

1. **an open eye vision**, where one gazes into the spirit realm while engaged in ordinary activities.

In Luke's gospel, the priest Zacharias had a vision. "When he came out, he could not speak to them. They realized he had seen a vision in the temple, for he kept making signs to them but remained unable to speak." (Luke 1:22)

In Acts 10, a Roman military officer named Cornelius had an open eye vision. One day around 3:00 p.m., he had a clear vision of an angel of God who came to him and said, "Cornelius!" The angel told Cornelius his prayers and gifts to the poor ascended as an offering before God.

The angel then told Cornelius to send men to Joppa to see Peter, who was staying with Simon the tanner in a house by the sea. When the angel left, Cornelius called two of his servants, told them what happened, and sent them to Joppa. (Acts 10:3-7)

Later, after having a *triple* vision showing Peter that God was no respecter of persons, Peter went to Cornelius' house and preached the way of salvation. All who heard believed and received the baptism in the Holy Spirit and baptism in water. (Acts 10:34-48)

One time in a restaurant, I experienced an open eye vision. The spirit realm opened. I saw the evil spirits operating in the lives of several people in the restaurant. Here, then, an open eye vision was coupled with discerning of spirits.

> 2. **an inner or spiritual vision**. One sees with the eyes of one's spirit.

During the night, the apostle Paul had a vision of a man of Macedonia standing and begging him, "Come over to Macedonia and help us." (Acts 16:9)

We saw previously in Chapter 11 that Paul was given a word of knowledge through this vision. Paul went to Macedonia by the will of the Lord and had tremendous ministry there.

> 3. **a vision while in a trance**. A trance is a state of suspended animation, like being frozen in time. A person is conscious but unaware of the activity around them as they gaze at something unusual or amazing in the spirit realm.

In Acts 10:9-10, Peter fell into a trance. Later, he said, "I was in the city of Joppa praying, and in a trance, I saw a vision . . ." (Acts 11:5)

While praying in the temple, Paul fell into a trance. He saw a vision of the Lord speaking to him, "Make haste and get out of Jerusalem quickly, for they will not receive your testimony concerning Me" (Acts 22:17).

In 1982 while in Jerusalem at the Museum of the Holocaust, I fell into a trance and saw a vision. I was standing and looking at one of the photographs of a concentration camp. Suddenly it was as though everything around me froze, and my inner self supernaturally went into the concentration camp in the picture. Just as supernaturally, about 45 minutes later, I found myself back in the Museum.

A lady named Candace was with me and had a similar experience. When we looked at our watches, we realized we had been in a trance for about 45 minutes. We were supposed to be back on the tour bus a half-hour earlier. Thank God for Carmi Roseman, our gracious tour guide, and a coach full of loving believers.

***

God still pours out His Spirit on everyone who believes. He is still blessing us with prophetic dreams and visions to help us know and fulfill His dream for us.

16

CREATIVE IDEAS

> You will keep him in perfect peace, whose mind is stayed on You because he trusts in You. (Isa 26:3)

God might speak to us personally by giving us creative ideas, i.e., divinely inspired thoughts of creativity.

In Isaiah 26:3, the Hebrew word for mind is *yester*. It means *concept*, *purpose*, and *creative imagination*. God will keep you in perfect peace when your mind and creative imagination stay on Him.

One creative idea from God is all you need to catapult your life into dynamic new levels of blessing. One innovative approach can be the next big thing to bless nations.

And the key to having a continuous flow of creative ideas is to keep our mind and creative imagination stayed on God.

Of course, not every good idea is a God idea. God's thoughts are good and perfect, not just good.

Creative Ideas

Every good gift and every perfect gift is from above, an comes down from the Father of lights with whom there is no variation or shadow of turning. (Jas 1:17)

So, find at least two to three Scriptures that support or confirm your creative idea. Pray over them. Do not proceed until the Lord gives you the green light.

17

RHEMA

> And take the helmet of salvation, and the sword of the Spirit, which is the word [*rhema*] of God. (Eph 6:17)

A rhema is:

- a *now* word from God
- a revelatory word quickened to your heart by the Holy Spirit
- *a living word from the written Word*—for a specific time and purpose
- the sword of the Spirit because the Holy Spirit inspires it
- God's Word coming alive to you.

For instance, you may have read twenty chapters in the Bible. Suddenly, you come across a verse that explodes with light and revelation. It precisely fits your situation. You might be listening to a message, and the same thing happens. You know God is personally speaking to you at that moment.

One time a minister friend of mine got a medical report that he was going blind. The minute he told me, I said, "How can you go blind with the light of the world in you?" God inspired that response. It was a Spirit-anointed word for someone who needed it right then. The proof was in the pudding - my friend did not go blind.

All it takes is one Holy Spirit-inspired word from the Scriptures to change everything

Jesus had fasted 40 days and nights and was hungry. The devil came, assaulting Jesus' soul with three strategically designed temptations. What do I mean by strategic?

After Jesus' baptism, the Holy Spirit descended upon Him like a dove. God's voice from Heaven proclaimed, "This is My beloved Son, in whom I am well pleased." Jesus then fasted 40 days and nights. After that, He was to begin his public ministry in Galilee. (Mt 3:16-17; 4:12)

So, the devil wanted Jesus to abort his ministry and his destiny to save the world.

The three temptations were:

1. to turn stones into bread to feed himself instead of depending on the Father;
2. to throw himself from the pinnacle of a mountain, in effect demanding the Father perform a miracle or send angels to save him; and

3. to forget about God's plan, serve the devil, and quickly possess the kingdoms of the world which Adam had forfeited to the devil. (Lk 4:5-6)

While these temptations were unique to Jesus, they fall into the same three categories of demonic enticements Adam and Eve faced, and we all face today: "the lust of the flesh, the lust of the eyes, and the pride of life." (Gen 3:6; 1 Jn 2:16)

Jesus destroyed each temptation by skillfully wielding the *sword of the Spirit* (Eph 6:17)—the Holy Spirit-inspired word from the Scriptures fitting the occasion.

To the first temptation, Jesus said:

> It is written, 'One must not live on bread alone, but on every word coming out of the mouth of God.' (Mt 4:4, ISV)

This was a Holy-Spirit inspired word (*rhema*) from Deuteronomy 8:3. It was the right word at the right time to stop the devil's temptation in its tracks.

With God, nothing will be impossible

Impossible is that which *seems incapable of being done, undertaken, or experienced.*

In Luke 1:35-36, Gabriel, the archangel, explained the seemingly impossible to the Virgin Mary. The angel told Mary that she would conceive the Christ child by the power of the Holy Spirit. He also revealed that her relative, Elizabeth, who was old and barren, was pregnant with a son.

He then said, "For with God, nothing will be impossible" (v. 37).

Mary joyfully received Gabriel's report. She said, "Let it be to me according to your word." The Holy Spirit then came upon her, and she miraculously conceived the Christ child. (v. 38)

Nothing is translated from the Greek *rhema*, which refers to the spoken word. No word spoken by God will ever be void of power or possibility of fulfillment!

***

So, fill your heart and mouth with God's Word – His life, light, truth, and overwhelmingly victorious point of view. Speak out the Spirit-anointed Word over life's circumstances. It will transport faith into your situations and effectively change them.

18

SONGS

> The Lord your God in your midst, the Mighty One, will save; He will rejoice over you with gladness, He will quiet you with His love, He will rejoice over you with singing. (Zeph 3:17)

God is love. He loves His redeemed people everlastingly. And He rejoices over us with singing.

Joy comes from the Lord

God is joy. In His presence is *fullness of joy*. (Ps 16:11) So, it should come as no surprise that God rejoices, yea, even sings powerfully over us.

Think about it: The Lord ever lives to make intercession on our behalf. Intercession includes singing, shouting, and rejoicing. (Rom 8:34)

God recreated us in the image of Christ, who *for the joy set before Him endured the cross*. (Heb 12:2) God delights in His new creation and wants us to rejoice and enjoy Him.

And God has given every Christ Believer the Holy Spirit—the Spirit of pure joy. The Holy Spirit helps us make melody in our hearts to the Lord and sing out joyful, spontaneous songs.

God inspires songs of joy

God inspires in us what He desires from us. I have written many songs to the Lord. When I sing to Him, He often gives me more joyous songs.

> For you are my hiding place; you protect me from trouble. You surround me with songs of victory. Interlude. (Ps 32:7, NLT)

Fresh, new songs should always be dancing around in our hearts, just waiting to be released through our lips.

Keep a praise perspective

Thank and praise the Lord with new songs—spiritual songs and songs with new words and melodies.

> Come on, everyone! Let's sing for joy to the Lord! Let's shout our loudest praises to our God who saved us! (Ps 95:1, TPT)

> Lift up a great shout of joy to the Lord! Go ahead and do it—everyone, everywhere! (Ps 100:1, TPT)

And, listen for His song back to you. For He rejoices over you with singing.

19

MINISTRY GIFTS

> That is why the Scriptures say, "When he ascended to the heights, he led a crowd of captives and gave gifts to his people." (Eph 4:8, NLT)
>
> Now these are the gifts Christ gave to the church: the apostles, the prophets, the evangelists, and the pastors and teachers. Their responsibility is to equip God's people to do his work and build up the church, the body of Christ.
>
> This will continue until we all come to such unity in our faith and knowledge of God's Son that we will be mature in the Lord, measuring up to the full and complete standard of Christ. (Eph 4:11-13, NLT)

God's Church

God's church consists of all people who receive and confess Christ Jesus as Savior and Lord and have been spiritually regenerated by the Holy Spirit. (Mt 16:16-19; Jn 1:12-13; 1 Cor 12:13)

The church is a living, spiritual organism. We are one body (the Body of Christ), born of one Spirit, with one head who is Christ. (Col 1:18; Eph 4:4)

So, when Christ ascended on high, He especially gifted some people to lead, build, and develop the Body of Christ. He called, anointed, and appointed some apostles, some prophets, some evangelists, some pastors, and teachers. (Eph 4:7-16)

The five-fold ministry have different functions

In a nutshell, apostles set direction. Prophets set in order. Evangelists preach the good news of salvation through Christ. Pastors feed, protect, and restore the souls of God's people. And teachers explain and make God's Word plain and practical.

Apostles

More specifically, apostles (*sent ones*) are God's special ambassadors or messengers sent to plant, establish, and strengthen churches.

The apostle works with the other ministry gifts to set in order gifts, services, and anything lacking or coming behind in local churches. (1 Cor 12:28; 1 Thess 3:10)

Prophets

Under divine inspiration, prophets speak forth the will of God to comfort, build up, and encourage people in God's plan and purpose.

As spiritual watchmen, they foresee, foretell, and forewarn God's people of spiritual storms. They tell God's people how to prepare for the same.

Prophets bring refreshing words from the Lord and exhort believers to deeper fellowship with God.

Evangelists

Evangelists are preachers of the good news of salvation through Christ. Their priority is to get people in right relationship with God.

Philip is the example of a New Testament evangelist. In his ministry, signs and wonders (healings, miracles, conversions) accompanied the preaching of the Gospel. (Acts 8:4-11; 26-40)

Pastors

Pastors were called shepherds in the Old Covenant. They feed, nourish, oversee, protect, and restore the soul of God's people.

The Lord, who is the Good Shepherd and Chief Shepherd, instructs shepherds to strengthen the weak, heal the sick, bind up the broken, bring back those driven away, and seek the lost. (Ezek 34:4; Jn 10:10; 1 Pet 5:4)

Teachers

Teachers explain and make clear and practical God's Word. The purpose is not to transmit information but transformational revelation. The teacher also leads and points believers to deeper fellowship with God.

Finally, it is clear that believers need impartation and training from all the ministry gifts. One gift alone will not equip or bring the saints to maturity.

What is the end goal of ministry gifts?

Conjointly, the work of ministry gifts is to:

1. Equip the saints for the work of the ministry. To equip means *to make fit or complete, restore, repair, prepare, completely furnish.*

2. Edify the body of Christ. To edify is to build up.

3. Speak the truth in love. God's Word is truth. (Jn 17:17). The spirit of the Word is love.

How long are these ministries in operation?

> till we all come to the unity of the faith and of the knowledge of the Son of God, to a perfect man, to the measure of the stature of the fullness of Christ (Eph 4:13)

Every believer needs to be part of a local church

The church is to assemble as one man. Assemble is *episunagogue*, a complete collection. Because it is a living organism, the church should have free-flowing services orchestrated by the Holy Spirit.

In the early church assemblies at Corinth, each one had a psalm, a teaching, a revelation, and interpretation. (1 Cor 14:26)

Certainly, every believer needs the corporate worship, prophetic revelation, vision, teaching, preaching, inspiration, training, oversight, fellowship, sharing of faith, time, talent, and treasures found in a God-honoring, Bible-believing, Holy Spirit-led and anointed New Testament local church.

Know who you follow

Like all believers, a minister's first calling is to be a follower of Christ. And, ministers are to be examples for all believers.

Respect and honor ministry leaders. Love and pray for them. But do not turn them into idols.

> Who is Paul, and who is Apollos, but ministers by whom you believe, even as the Lord gave to every man? (1 Cor. 3:5)

As always, test the spirits, whether they are of God. Never listen to or follow anyone who is not following the Lord. Those who speak for God will glorify the Lord.

Jesus says the sheep hear the voice of the shepherd when he calls, and they follow, but they refuse to follow a stranger because they do not recognize the stranger's voice. (*See* Jn 10:1-5)

God speaks to the world through His Church

The Church is God's oracle or speaking-place. We represent God in the earth. Timothy writes that the Church of the living God is the pillar and ground of the truth. (1 Tim 3:15)

The apostle Paul declares we are ambassadors for Christ to the world. And, at the same time, the church is making known to angelic powers the precious, multi-faceted wisdom and extraordinary plan of God through Christ Jesus, our Lord. (2 Cor 5:20; Eph 3:10)

20
CIRCUMSTANCES

> Now thanks be to God, who always leads us in victory through Christ. God uses us to spread his knowledge everywhere like a sweet-smelling perfume. (2 Cor 2:14, ICB)

A circumstance is an event or situation that causes or helps bring about the state of affairs in one's life.

Here, we will look at both challenging and favorable circumstances and how God speaks to us in and through them.

Circumstances of one's life can change for the better in a nanosecond

Some people have lived their entire life in difficult and challenging circumstances. That does not mean things have to stay that way.

Jesus encountered people who had all sorts of life-long misery. When he came across blind, disabled, and deaf people, He healed them. He told the poor they didn't have to be poor anymore. (see Luke 7:22)

So, there is hope for you, because God can change lifelong adverse circumstances in a nanosecond. Pray and ask Him to intervene in yours.

Circumstances of shut doors

Sometimes God uses events in our lives to get us going in a new direction.

Think of going on multiple job interviews without any open door for employment. While it might only be a matter of time before the right job opens up, it could also mean that God is shutting doors behind you so He can open a great door in front of you.

Circumstances where God guides, He provides

My trip to Israel is confirmed

The following events occurred years ago. But I share this story because it is a personal experience and one of my all-time favorites regarding circumstances that confirm God's will.

One night, while watching TBN, Paul Crouch spoke about a trip to the Holy Land in November 1982. I wanted to go. So, I called TBN for the tour packet, which I received near the end of October.

There were two drawbacks: (1) I didn't have $2,000 in cash to pay for the trip, and (2) the deadline had passed. So, I called Noseworthy Travel to see if I could use a credit card for the airfare. Yes, and there was room for 25 more people.

I then sent my entire paycheck to the agency, after which I was nearly broke. A few days later, however, I received a check in the mail for $500 for some legal contract services I performed months before. Now I could pay rent.

And, then, my employer gave me my vacation check, so I was able to pay bills that would come due while I was away.

From that point forward, money flew in. I got a refund check from a department store for $150. A few days before the trip, Liz, owner of a resale shop, came to my house with a $265 check from the store. She also bought a suit of mine for $200.

By now, I had replaced most of the money I paid Noseworthy Travel. Then, during the weekend before the departure, a friend of a friend called asking me to do her makeup for some big event. I earned $150.

With my credit card and cash, I thought I had enough money for the whole trip. I did not. There were out-of-pocket expenses—mini-tours, etc., I had not figured.

But one of the ladies who was sitting next to me on the flight from New York to Athens said, "Don't worry about it. I have plenty of cash." So, I borrowed $65 from her.

When I got back to Los Angeles, I had about $30. After arriving home and going through the mail, I found a check from the resale boutique for $150. Can you believe it? I just smiled and praised the Lord.

Most importantly, I had some amazing experiences on the tour. I was baptized in the Jordan River. The water was freezing, but that water baptism (my second) was phenomenal. And, I had an open-eye vision at the Museum of the Holocaust, which left me with an immense love and compassion for the Jewish people.

There is no doubt I was supposed to go to Israel when I did. Inner peace and joy, two or more Scriptures, several confirming voices, provision, and dynamic experiences substantially proved it.

What if there is no green light to proceed?

Anytime you do not have a green light on something, pray. Perhaps it is a matter of timing. But, if after praying the breath of God is not on it, leave it alone.

However, for those who like me have occasionally proceeded without a green light, or are tempted to do so, read more.

I have had all kinds of marketing gurus (masterminds) send me email blitzes to buy their training program. It is some once-in-a-lifetime opportunity: "I normally charge $100,000 for this program, but you can have it for $1,999." Like, $2,000 of my hard-earned money is chump change?

Recently, there was one that piqued my interest. I prayed about it several times. The breath of God was not on it. So, that was the end of that. That is until voices in my head kept telling me that maybe I was missing an excellent opportunity to learn more about creating wealth.

Fortunately, I know the difference between a mentally stimulating good idea and an anointed God idea. And I know how to cast down thoughts that oppose what God says.

When God says no, never let your soul (mind, will, emotions, desires, appetites) pressure you into going ahead anyhow. That is folly. If you are not sure, command your soul to be silent and wait for God to speak. Why not sing or shout out this Psalm?

> My soul, wait silently for God alone, for my expectation is from Him. He only is my rock and my salvation; He is my defense; I shall not be moved. (Ps 62:5-6)

When all hell breaks loose

You may be precisely where you are supposed to be, doing what you're supposed to be doing, when suddenly it seems as though all hell breaks loose.

For instance, I started writing this book at the end of December 2019. So, I also do contract work for a lawyer. His partnership broke up on January 3, 2020.

Then, two and one-half weeks later, I got the flu. I did wonder if my time on earth was up. For about a week, I was very sick and coughed for another two weeks. On top of that, I did not receive any payment from the lawyer for this year until March 11. And he only paid me about one-third.

Then, the government tells everybody to stay home because of the coronavirus pandemic. It's a good thing I had a few rolls of toilet paper because the stores in my neighborhood were continually out.

And it's a good thing I did not purchase that $2,000 marketing program a few weeks before!

Okay, so I'm trying to work at home. All of a sudden, there is drilling, banging, and sounding like an invasion from Mars outside my door.

It turns out, per an earlier notice, that the management scheduled *essential* repairs for the common walkway area on my floor. Brilliant! Let me add three weeks of earth-shattering noise while stuck inside to my list of not-so-fun events in 2020.

Yet, while circumstances have been off-the-chart crazy this year, I laugh a lot. I walk in supernatural peace and joy. And I know everything is going to be alright.

You see, while we may not like the inconvenience some circumstances impose, we can always rejoice in the Lord, especially when we know that we are right smack in the middle of God's good, acceptable, and perfect will. And we know *this too shall pass*.

Circumstances where God gets our attention
What role does the Church play in these perilous times?

As we said in the previous chapter, from God's point of view, the Church is His oracle or speaking-place, the voice of His Word, the pillar and ground of the truth. (1 Tim 3:15)

The Body of Christ is called to provide *essential* services to the world. We are the light to show the way and the salt to purify, heal, add flavor, and preserve life.

However, a compromising Church does not and cannot correctly represent Christ.

God is speaking to His Church to repent, get right, stay right, and be about our Father's business.

Stay on God's path

Do not be moved by circumstances. Pray for wisdom. Live by faith, that unfailing trust and confidence in God and His Word. Always show love. Hold onto your joy and peace. And do whatever the Lord tells you to do.

And when you don't know what to pray, pray in the Spirit. Trust the Lord, His Word, and His Spirit. Know that God is eternally good. And He is forever faithful.

The prophet Isaiah wrote for such a time as this:

> Even the youths shall faint and be weary,
> And the young men shall utterly fall,
> But those who wait on the LORD
> Shall renew their strength;
> They shall mount up with wings like eagles,
> They shall run and not be weary,
> They shall walk and not faint. (Isa 40:30-31)

God promises renewed strength to those who wait on the Lord. To wait is *to expect*, to *look eagerly for*, to *hope*. It also means *to bind fast, tie to, intertwine together like a tightly twisted rope.*

So, bind yourself together with the Lord like a tightly twisted rope in trust and dependency. In Him, you will find new strength, vision, provision, and continual hope for the future.

As we saw in Chapter 1, God's eternal Word is full of miracle-working, life-giving, situation-changing power. We need to lay hold to and say what God says in every area. Declare:

- The Lord is my shepherd; I shall not lack. (Ps 23:1)

- My God shall supply all <u>my</u> need according to His riches in glory by Christ Jesus. (Phil 4:19)

- And God is able to make all grace abound toward <u>me</u>, that <u>I</u>, always having all sufficiency in all things, may have an abundance for every good work. (2 Cor 9:8)

As God's child, you have His favor and His ear. (1 Pet 3:12)

Finally, God promises He will work out everything for the good of those who love and trust Him, the called according to his purpose. (Rom 8:28) Believe Him.

21

ANGELS

> Bless the Lord, you His angels, who excel in strength, who do His word, heeding the voice of His word. (Ps 103:20)

> Are they not all ministering spirits sent forth to minister for those who will inherit salvation? (Heb 1:14)

Throughout the Scriptures, we see angels sent from God ministering to God's people. Angels are spirit beings. When they manifest in the earth, they often look like ordinary men.

When Joshua was at Jericho, a man stood opposite him with a drawn sword. Joshua went to him and said, "Are You for us or for our adversaries?" The man answered "No, but as Commander of the Army of the Lord I have now come." (Josh 5:13-15)

David saw the angel of the Lord standing between earth and heaven, having a sword in his hand stretched out over Jerusalem. (1 Chron 21:15)

Gideon saw the Angel of the Lord face to face. (Judges 6:22)

When armies of Syria surrounded the house of Dothan where Elisha was, Elisha was calm because he saw into the spirit realm that the angelic armies of God outnumbered the Syrians. (2 Ki 6:15-17)

In Daniel, Gabriel the archangel appeared as a man and was called *the man Gabriel*. (Dan 8:15, 9:21)

At the first Christmas, messenger angels show up everywhere. They appear in visions and dreams, and in person. Sent by God, they speak on behalf of God. They come to encourage and aid God's people to fulfill His plan.

The angel Gabriel announces the birth of John

First, Gabriel announces to Zacharias, the priest, that Zacharias' aged and barren wife, Elizabeth, will conceive and bear a son. They are to call him John. And John, filled with the Holy Spirit from his mother's womb, will be a great man in God's eyes and turn many to the Lord. (Luke 1:11-17)

Gabriel visits Mary

Then, in Elizabeth's sixth month, Gabriel visits Mary, Elizabeth's cousin. Mary was a young virgin chosen by God to give birth to the Christ Child.

And having come in, Gabriel said to her, "Rejoice, highly favored one, the Lord is with you; blessed are you among women!" (Luke 1:28)

Gabriel continues:

> The Holy Spirit will come on you. The power of the Most-High will cover you. The holy Child you give birth to will be called the Son of God. (Luke 1:35 NLV)

> For with God, nothing will be impossible. (Luke 1:37)

Mary believed the words spoken by Gabriel. She said, "Let it be to me according to your word." Then, The Holy Spirit overshadowed her and the miraculous conception of the Christ Child happened. (Luke 1:38)

Finally, a messenger angel appeared to Joseph, Mary's fiancé, and assured him that Mary was pregnant by the power of the Holy Spirit. (Mt 1:20)

An angel brings good news of the Savior

When Jesus of Nazareth was born, an angel surrounded by glorious light appeared to shepherds in the fields, and said to them:

> Do not be afraid! For behold, I proclaim Good News to you, which will be great joy to all the people. A Savior is born to you today in the city of David, who is Messiah the Lord. And the sign to you is this: You will find an infant wrapped in strips of cloth and lying in a manger.

> And suddenly, a multitude of heavenly armies appeared with the angel, praising God and saying, "Glory to God in the highest, and on earth shalom to men of goodwill." (Luke 2:10-14, TLV)

Angels ministered to believers in the early church

> Now an angel of the Lord spoke to Philip, saying, "Arise and go toward the south along the road which goes down from Jerusalem to Gaza." (Acts 8:26)

An angel of the Lord spoke to Philip. The Scriptures do not say whether the angel appeared to Philip in a dream, vision, or in person. But the angel spoke clearly to Philip to take a specific route to Gaza: "Go toward the south along the road which goes down from Jerusalem to Gaza."

Philip immediately rose and followed the angel's instructions. By taking the route directed by God's angel, Philip's path crossed with the Ethiopian eunuch, a high-ranking official under Candace, the Queen of Ethiopia. The eunuch was on his way to Jerusalem to worship.

God set this up. The eunuch received Jesus Christ as his savior, was baptized in water, and went on his way rejoicing. And Philip was supernaturally transported to his next preaching assignment.

Angels delivered Peter

King Herod Agrippa severely persecuted the church. He killed James, the brother of John. (Acts 12:1-3) He then had Peter arrested and imprisoned with the intent of bringing him before the people after Passover.

In prison, Peter was bound with two chains between two soldiers. But constant prayer was made for him by the church. Just when Herod was about to bring him out, an angel of the Lord stood by Peter.

> An angel of the Lord came upon him, and a light shined in the prison; and he smote Peter on the side, and raised him up saying, "Arise up quickly." And his chains fell off from his hands. (Acts 12:7)

The angel led him out of the prison past the first and second guard posts, to an iron gate that led to the city. The gate opened to them of its own accord. They went out and down the street. Later, Peter realized he was not dreaming. This really happened.

***

While angels may manifest looking like mere men, they are far more powerful. One angel destroyed 185,000 Syrian soldiers. And in the future, one angel will bind the devil and throw him into the bottomless pit. (Isa 37:36; 2 Chron 32:21; Rev 20:13)

Finally, you may wonder how to distinguish the voice of the Holy Spirit from that of an angel. Think of it like this.

Angels

The Holy Spirit lives in your spirit. Thus, He speaks within. Angels are without, speak from without, and minister to your temporal needs.

22

FOUR STEPS TO CULTIVATE HEARING GOD

> And you shall seek Me, and find Me, when you shall search for Me with all your heart. (Jere 29:13)

Hearing God and developing intimacy with Him does not come by any formula. It evolves, over a lifetime, through much interaction with Him. Yet there are steps you can take to cultivate hearing God more clearly. Here are a few.

1. Get in the Spirit

In Revelation 1:10, the apostle John said: "I was in the Spirit on the Lord's day, and heard behind me a great voice, as of a trumpet."

Before John heard the great voice that sounded like a trumpet, he was in the Spirit. The first thing we must do to have higher spiritual perception is to get in the Spirit.

Break Away to a Quiet Place

Find a quiet place where you and the Lord can have undisturbed fellowship. You may have a prayer room, a spare bedroom, or an area under a tree in the back yard or in the park. Take your Bible along.

I like to spend time with the Lord first thing in the morning, while everything is calm, before the noise and busyness of the day set in. King David wrote:

> O God, You are my God. Early will I seek You. My soul thirsts for You. My flesh longs for You in a dry and thirsty land where there is no water. (Ps 63:1)

Focus on the Lord

Pray in the spirit for a few minutes. Concentrate on the Lord. Think about His majesty, excellence, greatness, goodness, grace, tender mercies, unfailing love, and great faithfulness.

Praise the Lord

Begin to wholeheartedly praise the Lord.

> Sing praises to God, sing praises! Sing praises to our King, sing praises! (Ps 47:6)
>
> Sing out the honor of His name. Make His praise glorious. (Ps 66:2)
>
> Sing to Him, sing psalms to Him. Talk of all His wondrous works! Glory in His holy name. Let the hearts of those rejoice who seek the Lord! (1 Chron 16:9-10)
>
> I will sing of Your power; Yes, I will sing aloud of Your mercy in the morning; For You have been

my defense and refuge in the day of my trouble. (Ps 59:16)

I will sing with the spirit, and I will also sing with the understanding. (1 Cor 14:15b)

In my experience, there is a *place* we can arrive through worshipping the Lord with singing high praises.

Suddenly, one is in the Spirit, in God's realm, in sync with Him. There is no concept of time, only an ensuing holy hush and a sense of His excellent majesty. We await His voice.

2. Expect God to speak

When you pray, keep a notebook and pen beside you. I have notebooks and pens everywhere—by the television, the telephone, my computer, my bed. Why? I am always expecting God to speak.

Wait and listen for God to speak

Listen for God's voice during and after prayer. Like the prophet Habakkuk, be alert to hear. Have a confident expectation that God will speak to you. And wait patiently to see what He will say to you (within you). (Hab 2:1)

Sometimes answers come to my mind before I ask the question. God said, "It shall come to pass before they call, I will answer; and while they are still speaking, I will hear" (Isa 65:24).

My personal prayer time is usually a synergy of praise, thanksgiving, petitions, intercessions, declarations, and decrees. Most of my inspirations come during these times with the Lord.

Expect God to speak to you through the Bible

As we saw in Chapter 1, the primary way God speaks to us is through His written Word, the Bible.

The Bible provides wisdom and answers for every aspect of life. It is a lamp to our feet (for today) and a light to our path (for the future). (Ps 119:105)

So, to understand God's perspective on everything, read and meditate on the God-breathed Scriptures. Keep the Word before your eyes and in your heart. (Prov 4:20-23)

The more you fellowship in God's Word, the greater will be your understanding of His will and perception of His voice.

3. Cultivate Hearing God by Listening for His voice throughout the day

God is always speaking to us. The Holy Spirit bears witness with our spirit to the truth of God's Word. Our conscience cheers us on to do the right thing. We know things intuitively.

Divinely inspired thoughts, explosive words, creative ideas, and prophetic dreams are normal. The fruit of the spirit—love, peace and joy—often lead us.

God may speak to us in an audible voice. The Holy Spirit may manifest in supernatural revelations, expressions and exhibitions. He may talk to us through a song He inspires in our hearts.

Other people may confirm what God has spoken to us. And, God will speak to us in and through all kinds of circumstances.

4. Be Continually Filled with the Spirit

The Holy Spirit is a fountain of life in the inner man. So, be continually filled, led and controlled by Him. (*See* Eph 5:18-21.)

***

I hope **the simplicity of Hearing God: 21 Ways God speaks to us** has ignited a passion in you to hear and know God like never before.

Epilogue

God loves to talk. So, He has filled the universe with His voice.

Remember the sound of God's voice

God's voice brings glorious light and truth to the world.

The Lord's voice comforts, encourages, and lifts us.

God's voice makes things crystal clear. He shows us the way. He corrects us when needed, yet always in love. The sound of the Lord's voice always leads us in triumph and victory.

Great peace, joy, and hope result from hearing and positively responding to God's voice.

God's voice will always draw you closer to Him. And He is as near as the whisper of His name.

***

Appendix 1A

Prerequisite to Hear God

Anyone can read the Bible and gain some knowledge of the truth. Open to Genesis 1, and you will discover that God created the world and every living thing.

Turn to John 3:16 and see God loves people so much that He gave His only begotten Son for us all. Whoever believes in Him will not perish but have everlasting life.

Indeed, everyone should read the Bible. Still, to see the big picture, connect truth, and grasp what God is saying, there is a prerequisite.

Jesus says, "You must be born again."

That is, you must be born from above, given a new spirit, spiritually regenerated by God's Spirit and God's Word! (Jn 3:3; Jn 1:13)

Why must you be born again?

- Because all have sinned and fall short of God's glory. (Rom 3:23)

Sin is an active rebellion in thought, word, and deed against our Creator. Sin separates us from God.

- to regain our likeness to God
- to get on the same road with God, spirit to Spirit
- to see, be in, experience the kingdom of God, and
- to know God and hear His voice.

What is the solution for sin?

Jesus Christ was crucified and died on the cross for us. His blood was shed for the sins of everyone. He is God's gift of salvation available to all. (Jn 3:16, Eph 2:8-9; Jn 1:12)

Receive God's gift of salvation

1. Believe in your heart that Jesus died for your sins and that God resurrected Him from the dead. (Rom 10:9)
2. Ask God to forgive you, come into your life, and make you a new creation.
3. Confess Jesus as Lord.

Seven fantastic results of your salvation

You are a new creation in Christ

Therefore, if anyone is in Christ, he is a new creation; old things have passed away; behold, all things have become new. (2 Cor 5:17)

You are now born again. You are a new creation. The Holy Spirit lives within you. (1 Pet 1:23; 1 Cor 6:19; Rom 8:11)

God has forgiven you
In Him we have redemption through His blood, the forgiveness of sins, according to the riches of His grace (Eph 1:7)

Sin is no longer your master
For sin shall not have dominion over you, for you are not under law but under grace. (Rom 6:14)

You have been delivered from darkness
God made us free from the power of darkness, and he brought us into the kingdom of his dear Son. (Col 1:13, ICB)

You are a child of God
Dear friends, now we are children of God. We have not yet been shown what we will be in the future. But we know that when Christ comes again, we will be like him. We will see him as he really is. (1 Jn 3:2, ICB)

You are accepted in the Beloved
to the praise of the glory of His grace, by which He made us accepted in the Beloved. (Eph 1:6)

You possess the kingdom of God
You have entered into the realm of God's rule and reign. While the full manifestation of God's kingdom is future, you have a foretaste of His kingdom within you now—

righteousness, peace, and joy in the Holy Spirit. (Rev 21:1; Rom 14:17)

Find scriptures that answer your need

Now, read and study the Bible to discover God's amazing promises and answers to every need. I would suggest you start with John's Gospel and then read all of the New Testament, and the rest of the Bible as you are led.

Connect with a local church

While many churches now live stream from the Internet, every believer should endeavor to be part of a good local church. You will find church leaders and others who will pray with you and help you grow in grace and the knowledge of our Lord.

***

You have embarked on the most excellent adventure of your life. May God's grace and peace be multiplied to you today and every day.

Appendix 1-B

About Bible Versions

The Levites preserved the Old Testament Hebrew text. The Lord's apostles quoted it, and we can entirely rely on it.

For the New Testament, copies of the ancient papyri in existence today are 95% alike. Minor discrepancies result from copyist spelling errors but do not alter the material text.

The Institute for Creation Research points out:

> The New Testament was written in first century A.D. There are some 25,000 early manuscripts in existence, almost 6,000 of which (many being only recognizable fragments) are Greek texts and the others being early translations of the Greek New Testament. The earliest textual evidence we have was copied not long after the original. https://www.icr.org/bible-manuscripts.

Today the most reliable English translations of the Bible are from the majority of the ancient Hebrew and Greek texts (the Byzantine family of manuscripts, or Received Text). The most literal word-for-word translations are KJV, NKJV, and NASB. I Believe one of these is essential for an in-depth study of the Scriptures.

Also available are thought-for-thought versions such as ERV, TLB, and NIV. Many consider these more comfortable to read. However, please realize they are paraphrases and not translations.

The failure of many modern versions of the Bible is they try to make their version conform to contemporary English. In doing so, they neglect the richness of the original languages.

To be a diligent disciple of the Lord, we must always seek to understand what God meant in the first place.

My personal favorite is the King James Bible, from which I received salvation as a child and from which I have studied for over 35 years. Habitually, I look up the Hebrew and Greek in a Concordance. I also read from an interlinear Bible. (An interlinear bible places the original language above the translated text.)

Then I sometimes compare 30 or more translations or paraphrases. If one of those versions makes the text clearer, then I use it in my books and booklets, in short blogs, and when speaking in a limited time frame.

For serious Bible study, however, one needs a literal word-for-word translation. After that, one can add a more comfortable to read version so long as it comports with the original text as expressed in the literal word-for-word translation, or as deduced after a study of the Hebrew and Greek.

Appendix 1-C

How to Rightly Divide God's Word

> Be diligent to present yourself approved to God, a worker who does not need to be ashamed, rightly dividing the word of truth (2 Tim 2:15)

It is essential that we rightly divide God's Word. To rightly divide means to cut straight. Here are seven guidelines to help you cut straight God's Word.

1. Live by faith in God through His grace

The foundation of the Old Covenant was the law and works. The basis of the New Covenant is God's grace—Christ Jesus.

The first five books of the Bible (Genesis, Exodus, Leviticus, Numbers, and Deuteronomy) comprise the law of God. The New Testament reveals the law was our schoolmaster to lead us to Christ. (Gal 3:24)

So, to make a straight cut of God's Word is to distinguish between law and grace. We keep the law in principle or spirit, we do not live by the letter of the law.

> But now we have been released from the law, for we died to it and are no longer captive to its power. Now we can serve God, not in the old way of obeying the letter of the law, but in the new way of living in the Spirit. (Rom 7:6, NLT)

In other words, there is nothing we can do to win favor with God. The only God-pleasing way to live is by God's grace through faith in Christ.

> For the law was given through Moses, but grace and truth came through Jesus Christ. (Jn 1:17)

> By grace, you have been saved through faith, and that not of yourselves; it is the gift of God. Not of works, lest anyone should boast. (Eph 2:8-9)

The Greek word for grace is *charis*. It means *benefit, favor, (free) gift*. Salvation and related divine resources and blessings are gifts from God. They are based solely on God's benevolence and the complete work of salvation by Christ Jesus. Salvation cannot be bought or earned – only received by the open hand of faith.

2. Do not spiritualize the text

Take the text as it is written. That is, receive the text in the usual sense of understanding. Someone said: "If the plain sense makes sense, seek no other sense."

3. Determine who is speaking, to whom, about what

The Bible records the words of God, angels, men, and the devil. We must know who is saying what to whom.

4. Discern whether a directive is specific to an individual or intended for everybody

The Lord invited Peter to step out of the boat and walk on water.

> So, He said, "Come." And when Peter had come down out of the boat, he walked on water to go to Jesus. (Mt 14:29)

The Lord spoke personally to Peter, not to everybody.

Here are four places you can confidently personalize scriptures:

Where God promises great blessing to "whoever" will receive it	e.g. Jn 3:16, John 1:12
In-Christ realities	Phrases referring to Christ, such as *in whom, by whom, through whom, of whom, in Him,* of Him, *by Him.* These that reveal the blessings, authority, and power every believer has in union with Christ.
Every place in the New Testament where a promise is made or a benefit is conveyed to believers	e.g. Rom 8:32 - "He who did not spare His own Son, but delivered Him up for us all, how shall He not with Him also freely give us all things?"

Every place in the New Testament where directions and instructions are given to believers.	e.g.: Eph 6:13 - "Therefore, take up the whole armor of God that you may be able to withstand in the evil day, and having done all, to stand."

5. Do not take scripture out of context

Read, study, and meditate on Scriptures in their setting or context.

6. Compare accounts

Compare the writings of the Old Testament prophets who lived in the same time frame. For instance, Zechariah lived around the same time as Haggai and brought a similar message. Micah lived about the same time as Isaiah.

Also, compare different accounts about an individual or an incident. For example, the story of Sennacherib boasting against the Lord and attacking Israel can be found in Isaiah 36-37, 2 Kings 18-19, and 2 Chronicles 32.

Read all four of the Gospels (Matthew, Mark, Luke, and John) to see the unique perspective each has.

7. Compare all the scriptures on a given topic

Study what the Word has to say on any given subject by comparing Old Testament scriptures with the New Testament.

If you follow these guidelines, you will do well in rightly dividing the Word of Truth.

God's Word is to be spoken and heard

Did you know in ancient times the Bible was not so much "read" as "spoken and heard"? That gives new meaning to the New Testament promise: "So then faith comes by hearing and hearing by the Word of God." (Rom 10:17)

Finally, Proverbs 4:20-22 says:

> My son, give attention to my words; incline your ear to my sayings. Do not let them depart from your eyes; keep them in the midst of your heart; for they are life to those who find them, and health to all their flesh.

***

Notes

Fox, Everett, *The Five Books of Moses: (The Schocken Bible*, Vol. 1 (New York, NY: Schocken Books, 1995)

Nelson, Thomas C., *Spirit-Filled Life Bible*, Third Edition (Nashville, Tn: Thomas Nelson, 2002)

Trench, R.C., *Synonyms of the New Testament*, Ninth Ed. 1880 (Grand Rapids, Michigan: Wm. B. Eerdman, 1947, reprint)

Vine, W.E., *Expository Dictionary of Old and New Testament Words* (Old Tappan, New Jersey: Fleming H. Revell Co., 1981)

Wuest, *Word Studies in the Greek New Testament*, Vol. 1 (Grand Rapids, Michigan: Wm. B. Eerdman, 1955)

Young, Robert, *Young's Literal Translation* (Public Domain)

Zodhiates, Spiro, *Hebrew Greek Key Study Bible* (Chattanooga, TN: AMG Publishers, 1991)

About Capazin Thornton

Capazin Thornton is a Christian speaker and writer. She is the author of *High Call to Pray, VICTORY 10 Keys to Living in Victory Every Day,* and *Christ Came to Save Us*. Capazin has a daughter and son, a wonderful daughter-in-law, and three amazing grandsons. She resides in Orange County, California.

Connect with Capazin

website:	https://capazin.com
blog:	https://capazin.com/capazins-blog/
	https://www.facebook.com/Capazin/
	https://www.instagram.com/capazin

Resources by Capazin Thornton

You may order these and other resources through:
https://capazin.com

VICTORY 10 Keys to Living in Victory Every Day is a compelling non-fiction book that inspires, encourages, challenges, and empowers readers to regain and maintain joyful dominion over life's circumstances. Rich in wisdom nuggets, simple, relatable life illustrations, and Bible promises, this book provides proven steps to help readers press through every test and trial to a state of triumph, light-heartedness, and joy.

<u>High Call to Pray</u>

is a uniquely powerful, concise, practical guide to help you pray more purposefully and effectively. You will discover many facets of prayer, prayer's real purpose, the character of God, the power of praying God's Word, the authority of the believer, the patience factor in prayer, and dynamic expressions of praise. And you will find 30 pages of Scripture-based, Holy Spirit-inspired prayers you can pray.

www.ingramcontent.com/pod-product-compliance
Lightning Source LLC
Chambersburg PA
CBHW070459100426
42743CB00010B/1679